A Kaleidoscope
of Children

A lens to
awaken a child's
mind !

~ Jayanti

A Kaleidoscope of Children

Jayanti Tambe

First Edition published globally by Read Out Loud
Publishing LLP in 2015

ISBN: 978-81-931360-4-1

Jayanti asserts the moral right to be identified as the
author of this work.

Thank you, Akshay for showing me through your growth and development just how magical a time one's childhood is. I am proud and grateful to be your mother.

My son, Akshay's artwork – a picture he created when he was just four years old.

"Spoon feeding in the long run teaches us nothing but the shape of the spoon."

-E.M. Forster

This book is also dedicated to my three mentors, Dr. M. Srinivasan, Dr. M. Horowitz, and Dr. E. Parnia, who over the past few decades have inspired me to grow and find my wings.

Srini, Michael, and Ezat, thank you for not spoon feeding me.

Contents

PHYSICAL DEVELOPMENT

"I'm ziggy-zag, I'm ziggy-zag, I'm cross..." **Looking at Outdoor Play in The Villages and Classrooms of South Africa**

"Open, shut them...open, shut them...give a little clap, clap, clap!!"
Looking at Hand Development in Young Children

"The hand is the cutting edge of the mind." - Jacob Bronowski
Whole Hand Development Leads to Whole Child Development

SOCIAL-EMOTIONAL DEVELOPMENT

What are little boys made of? "Snaps and snails, and puppy-dogs' tails." What are little girls made of? "Sugar and spice, and all that's nice."
Gender in Early Childhood

"...my dolls were as really children as I was myself a child." - Annie Besant
The Importance of Doll Play

REFLECTIONS ON TEACHING

FOREWORD

Holly Elissa Bruno

"We are knights. We protect the world."
-Pre-school child

CHILDHOOD IS A SACRED TIME. Do we honor our children's days as sacred? Or do we busy our children with lessons and recitals, play-dates and camps, tournaments and tutors? Do we test and evaluate our children, assigning them to confining categories, or do we allow each child to unfold into the unique person s/he is meant to be? Do we engage our children with conversation and play and exploration or do we allow them to lose themselves to a computer screen?

In childhood, very little is fixed and most things are fixable if we regain perspective. *Kaleidoscope* offers colorful prisms of needed perspective.

Wordsworth reminds us: *The child is father of the man.* Who your children are and what they experience of their childhoods significantly predicts their adult happiness. Who you were as a small child has much to do with how you navigate your world today.

By embracing the blessings and pitfalls of our early years, we discover choices about how to be with children. We can make changes for the better. Affirmed for what we are doing well, we can stretch into new dimensions of discovery with our children and with our own inner children. We can grow

1

with our children in healthy and healing ways. In short, we can have fun. Wonder. Amazement. Peace.

Turn the page of *A Kaleidoscope of Childhood* to begin the journey of discovery. Find out how to reinvent yourself as an adult guide for children. Find out how to transform your shortcomings into humor and your worries into creativity. Tambe helps us begin with the basics and build constructively from there.

Conkers. Sitting cook. Kabaddi. Four corners. These were the games of Jayanti Tambe's childhood. She played them with intensity across Mumbai, Bangalore and Pune. As an adult she has created and played games with children from India to California, South Africa to Louisiana. She has led teams at Pacific Oaks, Stanford and UCLA to co-create richly inviting learning environments for children to thrive as they grow.

Tambe's gift, which she passes on to her reader, is in seeing and sensing and appreciating each child in her native setting. With Jayanti Tambe's help, the South African child that has no tangible toys suddenly creates an orchestra out of found objects from the jungle. The inner city Los Angeles child who knows no safety can breathe and thrive in Tambe's playful and challenging spaces because the child himself created his safe and nurturing place. If you are like me, you will hear in Tambe's vivid vignettes a song to set your toe tapping with renewed energies.

Jayanti Tambe has written this book for you and for me. She wants to help us become better teachers, better parents and happier souls. Play is the answer. You say you don't know how to play? Don't have time? Don't believe adults should make fools of themselves playing like children? Tambe will call you out until you can't hold yourself back. There's too much fun waiting to be had. There's too much joy in your wings waiting to unfurl. Rumi exhorts: "You were not born to crawl."

Jayanti Tambe's *A Kaleidoscope of Childhood* offers our children and us a second chance at a happy childhood. This book is an honest, clear and no-nonsense guide to the childhood each child needs and deserves. *Kaleidoscope* generously:

- Lays out tools for adults on how to co-create learning environments with children.
- Offers practical tips on how to make something out of nothing.
- Names and comfortably addresses taboo topics like dying, sexuality, racism.
- Identifies assessment techniques to help us see possibilities we never envisioned.
- Adds dollops of children's words and wisdom.
- Captures in photographs the wonder of childhood.

Who should read this book? Are you:

- A teacher who's established that lessons work but no longer spark your imagination?
- An underfunded educator who can't afford supplies and equipment?
- An adult who knows how to work but not how to play?
- A stressed parent with just enough energy to cook for, bathe, protect and transport your children, but little left over for creativity?
- A person competent at navigating the adult world, but who feels out of place in a room bouncing with children?

Read this book to discover how much of the magic is in you, waiting to be released.

A Kaleidoscope of Children

Go ahead. Pick up *Kaleidoscope*. Begin the journey. Travel with Tambe. Hear the children's voices. Hear their questions, their concerns, their brilliance. Along the way, may you too find your pathway into and through that magical realm of childhood so that your travels this time can be rich, rewarding and fulfill your promise.

If you are like me, you may need to admit that you don't know everything about child development. In fact, I admit I am not a contender for mother, or teacher of the year! I made mistakes and had few role models. I didn't know I could ask someone I respected to be my mentor. I am of the generation of adults who thought we had to do it all and be it all. Those days are behind me now.

With helpful guides like Jayanti Tambe, I can see flowers abloom in a muddy March field. Rotate the *Kaleidoscope* in your hands. Allow yourself to see the endless permutations and combinations of color and shape and perfection that await you as a guide to the inner workings of young children.

Remember, children see themselves as: *Knights. We are knights. We protect the world.* May we, the adults, protect and honor and enliven their world so that children can freely and confidently and passionately venture into their worlds.

EVOLUTION

Dr. M. Srinivasan
(Founder and Principal, GEAR Foundation)

HAVE YOU EVER SEEN SOMETHING evolve in front of your eyes? The answer is generally 'No,' but I have witnessed it and have keenly observed it.

When I first met Jayanti Tambe in 1995, I was sure she had all the ingredients of a great mentor. Witnessing Jayanti crystallize her thoughts to become a pedagogue, was an astounding and transformative experience for me.

Jayanti willingly agreed to stand in as a teacher at GEAR in 1996, during very difficult times. I observed her to be a highly receptive and imaginative teacher who tried to implement a Gifted Education program. She caught on quickly and became an expert in incorporating the MI (Multiple Intelligences) concept at GEAR. She graduated to facilitating MI courses at De Anza College in the San Francisco Bay Area. This was her path for growth and preparation for a future career in education.

Once she started interacting with children at Stanford University's Rainbow School, she formulated ideas and interpretations of many useful world theories. Jayanti recorded anecdotes and blogs about the pain of reality and the pleasure of utopian thoughts. When she was in India with GEAR in 2013, the school that she was the director of was declared one of the top 10 programs in the country for respecting diversity. Her role changed from implementing to initiating changes on a large scale. She now holds the coveted position of executive director at UCLA Early Care and Education. What a journey!

I was not surprised at all; in fact it has been immensely satisfying to see Jayanti's potential bloom into an immense talent.

Her book gives an in-depth understanding of her learning and assimilation of the thoughts and ideas of several doyens of education, more specifically in the field of Early Childhood Education. The book may challenge the ideas and thoughts of many. That's what life is all about, isn't it?

Jayanti is the embodiment of sincerity of purpose and a model to many. Let the world start exploring ECE through Jayanti's thoughts!

INTRODUCTION

CHILDHOOD IS A MAGICAL TIME; a time when children are immersed in authentic play. When I think back to my childhood, growing up in Calcutta, I am reminded of this song: "If I could save time in a bottle..." If only I could!

I can't remember too much of the schoolwork I did when I was a young child; instead what I remember is this: playing with my dear friend, Raju. It's funny, but that's all I remember. We played. I could dedicate this book to my childhood that was so rich in play. We played cricket, we played football (soccer), we rode bicycles (the brakes didn't work – I remember that!) We played 'chor-police' (cops and robbers) and were often engaged in very muddy tournaments of kabaddi. I learned how to play conkers, and I was quite adept at spinning a top. We ran around like crazy, and climbed trees. We played a tame game called 'sitting cook' and a more robust one called 'four corners.' This was all in the span of the first seven years of my life. What a magical time that was.

I spent time in Mumbai, Pune and Bangalore and developed my true love for teaching. Two decades ago, M. Srinivasan (Srini) founder of GEAR school, introduced me to Howard Gardner's Theory of Multiple Intelligences.

I realized then that I truly wished to be an instrument to change the world of education.

Mahatma Gandhi rightly said, "You must be the change you wish to see in the world." In my opinion, true leaders embody visionary ideals and project themselves as agents of change. In the field of Early Child Education, a good leader is an advocate. She strives hard to work on behalf of not just herself, but also on behalf of others. Effective leadership, in my opinion, is a myriad of several qualities – inner strength, vision, collaborative spirit, cultural awareness, respect for diversity, collaborative vision.

I was just a young child when I first recognized the powerful impact educators could have on children. At this time, I lived in the city of Calcutta, and I volunteered at Mother Teresa's home. I observed how Mother Teresa worked with children, with compassion and love. The experience struck a chord in me that followed me into my current career as a preschool teacher, and as a community college professor in the field of Early Education.

I am extremely interested in the issues that impact children and families today. Our world is changing, and certainly, the demographics in our world are changing too. There is an overwhelming need for educators to understand and appreciate what families are going through.

Many of my friends have asked me who this book has been written for. This is a no-nonsense guide for parents of young children, on guilt-free parenting. Being a parent of a young child can be frightening, and even overwhelming. As parents, we pore over parenting guides trying to see if indeed our child fits into expected developmental domains. With children, however, there is no 'one-size-fits-all' formula. Children are different.

Parenting can be so satisfying and yet, in many ways, so difficult. I remember being criticized for giving my son a pacifier: "Take that piece of rubber out of his mouth!" I remember being ostracized in a classroom full of parents in the Western world for confiding that I had toilet trained my child at 18 months: "That is so developmentally inappropriate!" My friend was embarrassed because her husband carried their so-very-tall daughter in to and out of school. "Surely, she can walk and be independent," people criticized.

Many of us have been mortified as parents when our children are identified as the 'biters' in a classroom of toddlers; or when they 'lie' after having been caught bringing home someone else's toys. All these constitute the joys of parenting! Do children lie? Yes, they do. Do they bite? Yes, some certainly do. And do they throw tantrums? Oh yes, they do! Children do so much, and the important thing for parents and teachers of young children to know is that all of this is developmental, and that "this too shall pass!" Children in different cultures behave differently. Their families have different expectations of them. In the east, an inter-dependent relationship in the family is encouraged, while in the west, an independent one is considered the best.

Today's children live in a very different world. A world where they don't have so much of the outdoors; a world where homework is a part of their lives at tender ages; a world where iPads and Nintendos have hijacked them of their dreams and fantasies; a world where there is so much inequality; a world where, in fact, their childhood is being robbed from them. It's important for us to be able to return to children a life of authentic play – a life that is balanced, where there are judicious amounts of play interspersed with technology, a life in which a child can thrive!

I dedicate this book to childhood, and to children all over the world. I hope that this book gives parents and teachers a glimpse of how children develop, and helps them learn how it is possible to nurture their minds so that they grow to be happy and confident citizens of tomorrow.

PHYSICAL DEVELOPMENT

While there are three domains of development, it's very difficult to actually separate them from each other. When a child is engaged in play, you see all three domains of development: physical, cognitive and social emotional. Since a lot of physical development is covered in the chapters for cognitive development and social emotional development, this section is relatively small.

CHAPTER 1

"I'm ziggy-zag, I'm ziggy-zag, I'm cross..."

Looking at Outdoor Play in the Villages and Classrooms of South Africa

TRAVELING THROUGH SOUTH AFRICA HAS been such an opportunity for learning. While the classrooms themselves are really small, the outdoor spaces are huge, far exceeding the 1:75 sqft requirement of the State of California. Not all preschools have climbing structures: most have a lot of tires buried in the ground, or tires for swings... or even tires for steps, on climbing structures. At outdoor playtime, we saw children exit their classrooms in such a civilized manner – almost lining up to go play, a phenomenon that I have also seen in India. And once outside, they milled around, many of them choosing to just sit on the tires.

We think of the outdoors as just offering children physical, motor benefits. This could not be further from the truth. Children are developing in every way possible: physically, socially-emotionally, and even cognitively. We watched the children engaged in a very animated game of "I'm ziggy-zag." This is a game, akin to hopscotch, with different rules. Each square that you land on represents a category, and children are required to name items in the category as they hop on each square. For example, if they land on an 'animal' square, they recite the names of animals as they hop on each square. Once they complete the circuit, they land on each square with their eyes closed, saying, "I'm in?," and they are out if their feet touch the line. We watched, totally entranced as teachers and children went zigging and zagging through the squares, amidst lots of squeals and giggles. Organized games can be so much fun. There's so much learning there – physical, cognitive and social-emotional. We need more games like this one!

The truth is that preschoolers learn much through their senses, whether indoors or outdoors. In their environment, they get to touch things and learn through their tactile sense: it might be a squishy ball of play dough, or a crinkly dry leaf. They get to hear different sounds – the sounds in nature, of birds calling, of thunder rolling in the sky, or the sound of the gentle pitter patter of rain. They get to taste things – sometimes, they don't like how it tastes! These sensory experiences cannot be replaced by the technology of today. According to celebrated child development author, Rae Pica, "Children who spend a lot of time acquiring their experiences through television and computers are using only two senses (hearing and sight), which can seriously affect their perceptual abilities."[1]

Playing in an environment that is rich with what the 1970's architect Simon Nicholson called loose parts,[2] teaches young children how to appropriately deal with risks (alternating hands on a monkey bar, or walking on a log) and contributes greatly not only to children's enjoyment but also to building up their kinesthetic intelligence. When environments are set up with loose parts, they are more conducive to creative play. It was Nicholson's opinion that loose parts (rocks, stones, tree stumps, sand, fabric, twigs, wood, tires, balls of different sizes, logs of wood, and rope) empower children's creativity. Access to loose materials challenges children's motor skills, and improves their proprioceptive sense (the vestibular and proprioceptive senses tell a person where his or her body is in space and how and how much their muscles should react to different inputs). The proprioceptive system is strengthened by physical movements, like sweeping with a broom, hanging from monkey bars, or using a rope swing.

In 'Teaching Adults Revisited',[3] Betty Jones states that "young children, who haven't had enough experience to know what's safe and what isn't, are hard-wired for action." If children do not have the experience to test boundaries to understand what's safe, they do not have enough experience of thinking before acting. It's almost like they need to have some bright yellow caution tape to tell them that something is unsafe. This caution tape needs to be ingrained in young children, so they can practice with their bodies, and attempt challenging tasks. Their experience with developmentally appropriate risk taking allows their bodies to understand and gauge risks in their play as they grow and develop.

Looking at play from a statistical viewpoint, one comes to the dismal conclusion that there is not enough of it happening. While free, unstructured play is the best way to go, in the early years, *any* kind of play will do. Organized games are great fun, but children need a good balance of both structured and unstructured play. Children thrive in the outdoors, and need ample opportunities to practice using their large motor muscles. They need to run, jump, climb and hop, honing their vestibular senses as they play.

We didn't see enough of this, though every yard has the physical space required for large motor development. However, we did see some…and what we saw was truly unique, and very special. Some teachers whom we observed (especially at Matimu crèche) seem to have a keen understanding of this very basic need. The teachers get the children together in planned outdoor games, hula hoops and balance beams on a regular basis. Young children (even at age 2) practiced walking on balance beams, with bean bags on their heads. No, they were not getting ready for a modeling career; instead, they were preparing their bodies for growth and development.

So what needs to happen? Teachers need to go back to the basics. We need to offer children outdoor games that challenge young children – games that get their muscles to work. We need teachers like Magdalen – a teacher who is so innovative in the classroom. She used hula hoops to create an obstacle course of sorts where the children jumped from hoop to hoop, counting from one to ten. And she also used visual aids to help children "read" the numbers and understand one-to-one correspondence.

We need teachers like Tuli who added small bean bags to the children's heads as they balanced precariously on the balance beams, making the activity one notch more difficult for the children, scaffolding their learning in one smooth action! Looking at what Tuli did from the viewpoint of Vygotsky's scaffolding,[4] through the bean bag-balance beam activity, she created the zone of proximal development for the preschooler. Vygotsky described the zone of proximal development as the difference between what you can do alone unassisted, and what you are capable of doing under adult guidance or in collaboration with a more capable peer. In other words, a higher level of performance can be achieved when working with a more knowledgeable person.

We need teachers like Josephine and Lucky, who through their active music sessions, engaged a bunch of sixty preschoolers into moving their bodies in more ways than one can imagine. And we need gifted mentors like Frank, who are not afraid to stop teachers from making 3-year-olds sing the National Anthem and who, instead, get them involved in a boisterous and fun version of "Fire on the mountain, run, run, run!!"

The words "tsu-tsuma-tsu-tsuma" (run, run) will echo in my ears as I reminisce about the wonderful children engaged in just plain old outdoor fun…and as I reminisce, I will fervently hope for more!

Jayanti Tambe

"And oft when on my couch I lie,
in vacant or in pensive mood,
They flash upon the inward eye,
which is the bliss of solitude."
                                   -William Wordsworth, Daffodils

CHAPTER 2

"Open, shut them...open, shut them...give a little clap, clap, clap!!"

Hand Development in Young Children

WE TAKE OUR HANDS FOR granted. We do. As teachers, we see children work with their hands constantly: they open doors, play with blocks, and use forks and spoons. We are reminded then, of how useful our hands are. And that's what has been so disturbing here in South Africa and in many of the classrooms that I have visited in India. This ever-so-important use of our hands is mostly ignored in those preschool classrooms.

Children need manipulatives to work their hands. Manipulatives are tools that help enhance and strengthen a child's fine motor skills. They exist in most classrooms in the form of blocks, Legos, small cars, etc. By manipulating objects like blocks, or beads or cars, children develop better eye-hand coordination; their handedness (left or right) gets determined; and they are more prepared to hold a pencil and write in their elementary years.

So why was this happening? Why were there hardly any opportunities for hand development in these classrooms? When Todd and I observed the materials that were available for the children, we realized that there was really not enough stuff to go around: one box of pegs and two peg boards for the entire class; two pairs of kid scissors for 60 children...it was the same with all of the manipulatives.

18

So between not having enough material, and the apathetic attitude of the teachers, the children suffered, and continue to do so. Again, it's not easy to just watch, so Todd and I decided to create material for children to manipulate to increase their eye-hand coordination and to help with hand muscle development. We made peg boards from ceiling tiles and cars with washers for wheels. We created board games and dice, and we got the children child-sized brooms – anything to get those hands and arms, and upper body muscles moving.

There is a continuum in terms of hand development in young children, and it is this knowledge that helps teachers equip their environment in such a manner so as to enhance the process in young children.

When children begin to hold things, they begin with the fisted grasp. Between the ages of 1 and 2, young children tend to hold toys, pencils, crayons and other 'utensils' with their entire fist.

Then children move to the palmar grasp, around ages 2 and 3. It looks a bit opposite of the fisted grasp. The child's thumb will point down and the little finger will be up and off to the side. The child's elbow will also stick out to the side.

From the palmar grasp, young children aged 4 and 5 move on to the five fingered grasp, an immature grip. All five fingers are engaged in this grip, as the child uses four fingers to push a utensil against his thumb.

Most children reach a mature three-finger grip by age 5 or 6. In this hand-grip, a utensil is held between thumb, index and middle fingers.[5]

When children do not have anything to work their hands around, it's not just writing that suffers; everything is affected – physical/motor development, cognitive development and even social-emotional development.

Research[6] quoted by Christopher Bergland[7] in his blog suggests that creating a strong connectivity between both hemispheres of the cerebrum and both hemispheres of the cerebellum is key. This new research on the role of hand-eye coordination in the early development of toddlers is another clue for practical ways that we can give toddlers and children the best odds for learning and creating social connectivity, and also lay the neural groundwork for maximizing their potential. Bergland says, "These initial neural connections will play a crucial role in optimizing a child's human potential for a lifespan."

Play dough, small cars, balls etc. are necessary materials to help strengthen these neural pathways. The important push for the classrooms that we visited in these villages should be to equip the environment with materials that will help establish stronger eye-hand coordination.

What we are hoping that teachers here will realize, is that providing material to strengthen children's hand muscles does not have to break the bank. Even simple activities like getting children to put rubber bands on plastic bottles help to work their fine motor muscles and improve their eye-hand coordination. Daily activities should include cutting paper (if paper is available) or cutting and using play dough (which can be home made), tearing and crushing paper, using tongs or tweezers – basically actions that require the fingers to work with the muscles of the hands.

Easels (even writing pads) affixed to the walls should also be in each classroom. While we give children a lot of drawing and writing on papers on a table/surface, we neglect the value that easels provide. When a certain amount of body stability has developed, the hands and fingers begin to work on movements of dexterity and isolation as well as different kinds of grasps. Children will develop fine motor skills best when they work on a vertical or near vertical surface as much as possible. In particular, the wrist must be in extension.

Hopefully, by incorporating more and more fine motor activities into their daily curriculum, teachers will see the many benefits that accrue from this – children will very successfully be in their continuum of hand development, stepping ever closer to reading as well as writing.

"Listen to the musn'ts, child. Listen to the don'ts. Listen to the shouldn'ts, the impossibles, the won'ts. Listen to the never haves, then listen close to me...anything can happen, child. Anything can be."

-Shel Silverstein

CHAPTER 3

"The hand is the cutting edge of the mind."

-Jacob Bronowski

Whole Hand Development Leads to Whole Child Development

OVER MANY YEARS OF WORKING with children, i have watched as children used their hands in different ways: some painted with them, some used their hands to mold play dough, and some used their hands to pick up crayons and chalk. There is in fact a continuum in muscle development in young children.

- Whole arm
- Whole hand
- Pincher
- Pincer

According to authors J. Michelle Huffman and Callie Fortenberry,[8] writing progress depends largely on the development of fine motor skills involving small muscle movements of the hand. They state that muscle development for writing is a comprehensive process that begins with movements of the whole arm, and progresses toward very detailed fine motor control at the fingertips.

They outline four stages of fine motor development, which set the stage for early writing success: whole arm, whole hand, pincher, and pincer coordination. Fine motor development, they say, begins with strengthening and refining the muscles of the whole arm. They add that this full arm movement (that we see in infants) is a precursor to muscle development of the hand. During infancy, babies' hands are usually clenched in fists. Their finger movements are very limited. Babies use a 'palmar grasp' the grasp that you see when they close their hands and grip your finger. In the first few months of a baby's life, the hand and arm movements develop rapidly. Children develop motor skills from the center of their bodies, outwards ('proximal to distal'). This means that babies first manage to control their upper arms and legs before they can gain control over their fingers and toes.

Young children then transition to the building of the muscles of the whole hand. J. Michelle Huffman and Callie Fortenberry further state that strengthening the hand muscles leads to the ability to coordinate the finer movements of the fingers. Children then develop the pincher movements by pressing the thumb and index finger together.

We see the progression of hand development in the grips that young children use to hold a pencil. Typically, children begin with the fisted grasp and then move to the palmar grasp to hold a pencil. They then progress to holding a pencil with the '5 finger' grasp. As they refine their grasp, children finally begin to hold pencils with the 'three finger' or tripod grasp.

- Fisted grasp: This is when a young toddler uses the entire upper body or shoulder muscle to hold and move a writing implement on paper.
- Palmar grasp: Children then begin to use a palmar grasp where they use the strength of the upper arms to hold and move a crayon or a pencil.
- Five finger grasp: This is very common in the preschool years where children tend to hold writing

instruments with all five fingers. They use the muscles of the wrist to make markings or drawings with pencils and crayons.

• Tripod grasp: This a mature grasp that older preschoolers are able to use, where they can hold a pencil using three fingers (the thumb, the index finger, and the middle finger.

Another aspect that we see in early childhood is hand dominance. Nearly all fine motor activities, including cutting and writing, require a dominant hand (being left-handed or right-handed) and a non-dominant hand. Hand dominance, as the article states, can be seen as early as age 3 or 4, although it may not be firmly established until a child reaches age 6 or 7. Once a child becomes comfortable with one hand as the dominant hand, the remaining hand becomes the non-dominant hand by default. While the dominant hand performs tasks such as using a pencil or scissors, the non-dominant hand acts as the stabilizer. For example, one hand holds the scissors when cutting, while the other hand moves the paper.[9]

The more delicate tasks facing preschool children, such as writing or tying shoelaces or even buttoning up pants, represent a challenge for many young children. In the article, *'Fine Motor Skills - Infancy, Toddlerhood, Preschool, School age, Encouraging fine motor development'*,[10] the author states that the central nervous system is still in the process of maturing sufficiently for complex messages from the brain to get to the child's fingers. The author stresses that these small muscles tire more easily than large ones, and the short, stubby fingers of preschoolers make delicate or complicated tasks more difficult.

There are many things that we can do as educators and as parents to encourage hand development in young children.

- Provide vertical or inclined surfaces to work on. In this position, the wrist is properly positioned to develop stability and skillful use of the finger muscles. In this grip, children tend to use one hand as a "stabilizer" and the other hand to write with. Vertical surfaces also encourage the proper positioning of the arms and shoulders for work.
- Instead of giving children markers, give children crayons to use. Markers glide too easily on paper, and produce bright colors without too much effort. Children build muscles when they use crayons or chalk to make impressions on paper.
- Play dough or even the dough used to make 'rotis' can be given to facilitate fine motor development in preschoolers.
- Paper tearing encourages fine motor skills in young children.
- Spray bottles, eye-droppers and pipettes are great for encouraging fine motor development in young children.

The development of strong fine motor skills is essential to complete preschool tasks like tying shoelaces, buttoning clothes, and holding a spoon. In the later years, hand development is necessary for tasks such as writing and cutting with a pair of scissors. When children's fine motor skills are not well developed, they may have difficulty learning to write and they may struggle with some of the day-to-day critical tasks in their kindergarten years.

"There is in every child at every stage a new miracle of vigorous unfolding."

-Erik Erikson

Alternating hands on a monkey bar teaches young children how to appropriately deal with risks.

Access to loose materials challenges motor skills and improves proprioceptive sense.

By manipulating objects like blocks, beads or cars, children develop better eye-hand coordination and they are more prepared to write in their elementary years.

Children thrive in the outdoors and need ample opportunities to practice using their large motor muscles. They need to run, jump, climb and hop, honing their vestibular senses as they play.

Children will develop fine motor skills best when they work on a vertical or near vertical surface as much as possible.

Fine motor development begins with strengthening and refining the muscles of the whole arm.

When cutting with scissors, the dominant hand performs tasks such as using scissors; the non-dominant hand acts as stabilizer.

When writing with a crayon, the dominant hand performs tasks such as using the crayon; the non-dominant hand acts as stabilizer.

By manipulating objects like balls and paintbrushes children develop their handedness left or right.

Children develop motor skills from the center of their bodies outwards 'proximal to distal'.

Stretching to paint at an easel is also about development of muscles.

Access to loose materials challenges children's motor skills.

Children also need organized outdoor play for lare muscle development.

Play activities such as painting provide for children's fine motor development.

Spray bottles are great for encouraging fine motor development in young children.

SOCIAL-EMOTIONAL
DEVELOPMENT

It is in the early years that children first make sense of who they are. They learn to understand their emotions: what makes them feel good about themselves, and they learn to build relationships with other children and adults. Children at these young ages also learn to understand, manage and articulate a range of feelings, from happiness to frustration, from sadness to excitement.

Theorists and philosophers have delved into this topic to better understand how young children grow and develop socially and emotionally. Having spent some time working in three countries, India, USA and South Africa, I was able to get a wider view of how these diverse cultures differ in this realm of development.

Todd Hioki, my colleague and I were both Fellows with the "Teach With Africa" program. We visited many classrooms, and worked with the teachers and children in the villages in rural South Africa. The following chapters outline social-emotional development, with a closer look at the development of children in South Africa whom I had the privilege of working with.

CHAPTER 1

What are little boys made of? "Snaps and snails, and puppy-dogs' tails." What are little girls made of? "Sugar and spice, and all that's nice."

Gender in Early Childhood

As a child, I spent hours playing with dolls made of plastic, paper and cloth with my cousin Sushi, and with my dear friend, Sharmila. Those were the days in India when boy dolls didn't exist in stores. We had girl dolls – plenty of them. And yet, the games we played were the same as the ones that children play today: our dolls got married, dressed in colorful bits of fabric or paper made into sarees, with jewelry and flowers in their hair. And they were married to the stuffed animals that we had. In fact, our favorite was the stuffed cat – he made a great bridegroom.

Today, many decades later, there is a definite understanding of what boys and girls are made of. Much as they make adults uncomfortable, today's preschool educators use anatomically correct words to describe the differences between boys and girls. And they use anatomically correct dolls too. That's where the brouhaha starts. Laura Coffey, in her article on this subject[11] writes, "For decades, baby dolls have been famous for their vagueness. Are they girl babies? Are they boy babies? Really, without their pink or blue outfits, who could say?" Of course, this doesn't apply to Barbie dolls, who don't fall into the category of 'vague', or for that matter, into the category of 'baby dolls'. In fact, the doll, despite its disproportionate figure, is all 'girl' doll, and Ken, a boy doll.

Parenting experts like Dr. Michele Borba[12] say it's important for parents to use the correct names for male and female body parts with their children. "At ages 3, 4, 5, we should be talking to them with anatomically correct words: penis instead of pee-pee… You don't do that with other body parts. You don't call it your 'elbow-y' or your 'toe-toe' … We've learned that if parents are relaxed about this when kids are younger, then the child will feel comfortable coming to you with harder conversations later."

I'm sure that, looked at through a cultural lens, this would make many educators and parents uncomfortable. "Do they really have to use those words?" I have been asked that several times. I know several educators in India who would think twice about having anatomically correct dolls in their classroom. So rather than this being a child development issue, it really becomes a cultural and value-based issue. The jury is certainly out on this one. So far we have asked, "What are you comfortable saying? If it makes you uncomfortable, don't. You have a choice." However, with the increased awareness of crime in our world today, we might have to look at how these issues are addressed more closely.

Gender is a taboo subject, especially in India, and in many other Asian countries. Adults are uncomfortable discussing this topic, and even more reluctant to speak of it with young children. This needs to change. According to the National Crime Records Bureau, the number of child rapes registered in India increased by 30% between 2010 and 2011 when 7,112 cases were registered. Children are not educated on topics like child abuse, and when it does happen, they are scared and reluctant to discuss it with their families, or with a school authority. "Sex is such a taboo word in our society that we don't allow our children to talk about it," says Aruna Broota, a clinical psychologist based in New Delhi. Sameer Malhotra, a mental health specialist adds, "Children are often reluctant to discuss sex abuse with their parents as they are unsure how their parents will react."[13]

It is time to sit down and have real conversations with children about their bodies.

Tips to talk to your children about inappropriate touching:[14]

1. Your body is your own.
2. Good touch / bad touch: recognizing inappropriate touching.
3. Good secrets / bad secrets: Every secret that makes a child anxious, uncomfortable, fearful or sad is not good and should not be kept.
4. Prevention and protection are the responsibility of an adult. Adults should avoid creating taboos around sexuality, and make sure children know whom to turn to, if they are worried, anxious or sad.

In many cultures around the world, there is definite gender segregation in families. Many of these families, because of this gender segregation, may experience violence and abuse within the homes. These families may in turn not accept the occurrence of sexual violence or that any form of abuse (verbal, sexual, physical) of children actually occurs. Oftentimes, these young children (girls) live in cultures that define them not by who they are, and what they might achieve, but by the male figures in their lives (fathers, grandfathers, uncles, cousins and siblings.) This suppression of reality as well as ignorance about sexual matters needs to change. Families need this information, parents need this information, and, young children need this information as well.

It is time for us to be educated and to stop the exploitation and abuse of young children. It's time to talk with children to let them know that we are there for them. It's time for children to be educated about their bodies, and their rights regarding their bodies.

"History will judge us by the difference we make in the everyday lives of children."

-Nelson Mandela

CHAPTER 2

"...my dolls were as really children as I was myself a child."
-Annie Besant

The Importance of Doll Play

THERE IS SOMETHING JUST MAGICAL and mesmerizing about watching children play. I think that I could do it all day. During one of Todd and my visits to a rural school in South Africa, we set up the classroom and observed a group of little girls walk to the dress-up area and make a beeline for the baby dolls. I watched, completely transfixed, as a little girl deftly fastened a baby to her back using her sweater – just as her mother must carry her babies.

There was something truly beautiful about the whole thing. And it took me back down memory lane. I played with dolls from when I was very small, until I was fourteen. My dearest friend, Sharmila (whom I have mentioned before) and I played with plastic dolls, while my cousin Sushi and I played with paper dolls. Our dolls were extensions of ourselves, and they did things we couldn't. Our dolls traveled the globe, wore 'fancy' clothes, and lived amazing lives while we watched and lived through them vicariously.

My son also played with dolls – he played with GI Joes since that's what he liked. (We threw away the weapons so they were merely 'boy' dolls) The GI Joes came camping with us wherever we went. They had tiny tents, sleeping bags, pillows and even blankets. And my son just loved his dolls.

A Kaleidoscope of Children

Watching my son when he was little, and now, watching the children bond with their baby dolls reminded me of John Bowlby's attachment theory.[15] Bowlby believed that the "…earliest bonds formed by children with their caregivers have a tremendous impact that continues throughout life." He suggested attachment also serves to keep the infant close to the mother, thus improving the child's chances of survival.

Children begin to play with dolls early, as early as around 18 months of age. As they grow older, their play becomes more symbolic. Another factor that helps with their dramatic play is that children begin to imitate behaviors. Thus their play takes on stories, as children watch their parents and caregivers each day.

"Pretend play, (of which dolls are a part)"…, according to experts, "…benefits all areas of development….by dressing and feeding dolls, children enhance fine-motor skills. By assuming roles and interacting with other children, they practice language and social skills, including sharing, cooperation, helping, and problem solving. They learn the different roles people play and begin to see their own place in the world."[16]

Children have a fundamental need to bring the large, loud world into manageable size, according to Jerome Singer, psychology professor at Yale University (1994).[17] In his research, Singer found that, "compared to night dreams, practically no significant research had explored daydreams or awakening imaginative thought systematically or experimentally." His subsequent research work showed that "…adults with test scores suggesting a fairly rich fantasy life were better able to control their movements and compulsive behaviors compared to others lacking evidence of such imagination. [Children] who showed more evidence of richer fantasy lives more capably restrained compulsive acts."[18]

Pretend play gives a child a miniature world where he or she is the mother or the father, and all of the toys manageable and easily manipulated. A sense of control in this kind of play helps children navigate through their childhood problems. As the experts in child development state, "[A child] can come to grips with what are often major crises, such as a battle over feeding or messy toileting, by 'writing' the scenarios herself and putting dolls into the now miniaturized situations and experiencing the power of watching them suffer as she pretends to be Momma."[19]

Another very important thing that children learn while playing with dolls is the ability to empathize with their peers. Today, more than ever, as educators, we focus on this facet of development. Empathy helps children make wise decisions, resist peer pressure (especially in later years, when bullying becomes a reality in school), and have better social interactions. Playing with dolls helps to hone a preschooler's social skills. They pretend and play-act scenes with their dolls, demonstrating the ability to understand and appreciate the perspectives of others. This kind of play helps move a child away from egocentric thinking. "Egocentrism refers to the child's inability to see a situation from another person's point of view. According to Piaget, the egocentric child assumes that other people see, hear, and feel exactly the same as the child does." Children show the ability to take turns, and learn and appreciate the ideas and opinions of others. So, let the children play with their dolls. As Fred Rogers says, "Play is often talked about as if it were a relief from serious learning. But for children play is serious learning. Play is really the work of childhood."

> *"There should be a place where only the things you want to happen, happen."*
>
> -Maurice Sendak

CHAPTER 3

Pink is a girl color...or is it?

Exploring Gender Bias in the Preschool Environment

WHEN VISITING PRESCHOOLS IN THREE countries, USA, India and South Africa, I have seen every hue and shade of pink and purple. What I have observed, especially in South Africa, is that boys and girls are both dressed in these shades – there is no discrimination of color. I was transported back to around 15 years ago, when I had bought a lovely purple fleece for my then 10-year-old son. It was warm and fuzzy and functional. There was no gender bias in our home in terms of color or toys. And my son wore his jacket quite happily till he entered a school in California. A couple of weeks in the cold San Francisco Bay weather brought out our jackets, and my son would proudly zip up his purple fleece and head on to school.

A few weeks into winter, I got a call from a dear friend who insisted that I go shopping with her for a jacket for my son. "He has one already," I argued. "But it's *purple*, a *girl* color. The children are teasing him about it." And that was that. No more purple and pink in our home for the boys after that. Looking at how the boys in South Africa were dressed in just those colors made me wonder if indeed this preference in terms of gender is determined by our genes, by poverty, or if it is just cultural. There are of course, divergent views regarding the reason for this color choice.

Is pink a choice that a baby or a young girl makes, or is the choice of the color an adult one? Claudia Hammond, in her article, "*The Pink Vs. Blue Gender Myth*" states that cultural norms may also shape color preferences. She adds "in cultures where pink is considered the appropriate color for a baby girl and blue for a baby boy, babies become accustomed from birth to spending time wearing or even surrounded by, those colors. This makes it hard to know whether any preferences expressed later on are hard-wired."[20]

Philip Cohen, sociologist at the University of Maryland adds to this by stating, "This happened during a time when mass marketing was appearing. Being 'gender normal,'" he stresses, "is very important to us, and as a marketing technique, if retailers can convince you that being gender normal means you need to buy a certain product — cosmetics, plastic surgery, blue or pink clothing, etc. — it just makes sense from a production or mass marketing perspective."[21]

Although the 'pink is for girls' bias was not present there, when I spoke with a couple of men in South Africa, they were both of the opinion that *only* girls should play with dolls, and that boys should never play with them. This attitude seems quite pervasive and the dramatic play areas in almost all of the schools (co-educational schools for both boys and girls) had similar toys/props: baby dolls, clothes to dress the dolls in, doll beds and blankets, kitchen toys, and in one preschool, some "doctor" dress up clothes. Again, my curiosity got the better of me. I wondered if this too is a genetic choice or if we as a society, influence boys and girls in terms of the toys they play with. There is some very interesting research on this topic too. When offered the choice of playing with either a doll or a toy truck, girls will typically pick the doll and boys will opt for the truck.

In her book, '*Children in Globalising India: Challenging Our Conscience*', author Enakshi Ganguly Thukral highlights this plight of girls in India and the inherent bias surrounding the female gender in countries like India. She states, "At home, the daughter is groomed by her family and prepared for the only function in her life: to be a good wife and mother." Socialization in this culture, she adds, "…begins with gender specific toys: dolls, kitchen sets for girls and outdoor games, medical kits etc. for boys."[22]

This isn't just because society encourages girls to be nurturing and boys to be active, as people once thought. At least in terms of play in rural South Africa, I have seen children, both boys and girls, playing with each other. We haven't heard or seen the equivalent of "you can't play with us; you're not a girl." Children in India and in South Africa, although they are dressed in pinks and purples alike, seem to show very little gender bias at a young age when it comes to play.

However, the issue of gender is very important in early childhood, and it is where conversations regarding gender should begin. Authors Olaiya E. Aina and Petronella A. Camero, in their article on gender, '*Why does Gender Matter?*' state, "Almost immediately after becoming gender aware, children begin developing stereotypes, which they apply to themselves and others, in an attempt to give meaning to and gain understanding about their own identity." Girls and boys seek out friends of the same gender as they grow older. "These stereotypes are fairly well developed by 5 years of age, and become rigidly defined between 5 and 7 years of age, making the preschool years a critical period to deal with gender stereotypes."[23]

William wants a doll, but his father doesn't want to buy him one. Finally, his grandmother comes to visit — and at last William is understood. She gets William the doll (he "loved it right away"). And she explains to William's father (who "was upset. 'He's a boy!' he said / 'Why does he need a doll?'")

Why William needs it:

44

"so that when he's a father like you, he'll know how to take care of his baby and feed him and love him and bring him the things he wants, like a doll so that he can practice being a father."
-Charlotte Zolotov, *William's Doll*[24]

CHAPTER 4

"It has been a terrible, horrible, no good, very bad day....or has it?"

-Judith Viorst

Another Look At Children And Temperament

THERE ARE SEVERAL MONDAY MORNINGS when I have what author Judith Viorst calls a "terrible, no-good, very bad day." It is never a good idea to come anywhere near me on those days. And definitely not before I have had several cups of very strong coffee.

Yet, in preschools, both in India and in South Africa, I have not often seen children who seemed to have those kinds of days. I have seen happy children. Very happy children. I have spent time with placid children. And I have seen content children. This surprised me, and I began to think of children and temperament.

A child's temperament can be described as the manner or way in which he/she reacts to different stimuli and events in his/her world. Children's temperaments are defined after closely examining several traits. Thomas and Chess in 1977[25] stated that every child is born with a set of personality characteristics, i.e. their temperament.

Based on these traits, researchers generally categorize children into three temperament types:

Easy or flexible children tend to be happy, regular in sleeping and eating habits, adaptable, calm, and not easily upset.

Active or feisty children may be fussy, irregular in feeding and sleeping habits, fearful of new people and situations, easily upset by noise and stimulation, and intense in their reactions.

Slow to warm or cautious children may be less active or tend to be fussy, and may withdraw or react negatively to new situations.

When interacting with children in both countries, I have observed that on the face of it, they all seem to be very easy, flexible children. I am yet to come across a feisty one (in school; at home, the story is always different. Children behave "normally" at home, and may appear to be difficult or feisty, or in fact, in some situations, even slow-to-warm-up.). I have seen children sleeping in a room full of activity, in a room full of the noises of children playing, and in a room with the hubbub of adults talking to each other. These infants seem to be able to calm themselves and continue sleeping through the mayhem. This made me wonder – is temperament influenced by culture?

Cultural influences affect the personality of humans in several ways. The effect of culture can be seen individually in children. Looking at children from an ecological theory perspective, Urie Bronfenbrenner suggested that the family, the school, the church, culture and values, and the interaction between these entities affect children.[26] Any change in any of these ecosystems causes a ripple effect that shapes the individual.

Larissa Gaias[27] et al expanded on Bronfenbrenner's theory to coin the term, 'developmental niche', a term used to describe how a child's environment is shaped by culture. According to Gaias et al, the developmental niche contains three components: the physical and social settings of the child's life, culturally regulated practices of child rearing and care, and the psychology of the caretakers. These three components interact with one another, and with the child, to account for individual differences. This is why we see differences in personality, or as in the case of what I have observed in classroom settings in India and in South Africa, this may be why we see "similar" temperaments in young children.

Parenting takes on a different note as cultures differ. In the west, individualism and independence is encouraged, and very young children are allowed to decide for themselves when they are "all done." In countries like India and South Africa, however, a more collective way of life exists, where children and their caring adults form a symbiotic relationship. It's not unusual to see children being spoon-fed or carried although they may be able to walk or to feed themselves.

In both India and in South Africa, I have seen children in the morning at drop off: they come in calmly and happily. When they are in a group, they seem quiet. They form lines (obediently, almost submissively) to go to the bathroom; there's no pushing and shoving. If there is any pushing or shoving, it's minimal, and often nipped in the bud by the teachers and caregivers. The children do not seem to fight with each other. Although toys are few and far between, there's no snatching and grabbing. Children get fed their meals. There's minimal fussing, and very few "all dones."

It is quite surprising that we saw easy or flexible children in cultures in India and South Africa. From the western viewpoint, children are not always 'easy'. Transitions from caregivers or parents, or the sharing of a coveted toy makes children react and behave differently. Yet, during our observation of children in South Africa, we saw fewer variations from 'easy and flexible' children. We observed them at meal times, at naptime, at drop off times...only not at pick up times. Authors Allard and Hunter emphasize that, "It is important to understand that although a child's basic temperament does not change over time, the intensity of temperamental traits can be affected by a family's cultural values and parenting styles."[28]

For the most part, I have seen happy children in both Indian and in South African childcare settings. This is however just the tip of the iceberg. There is so much to study about the topic of cross cultural temperament development, but it's important to understand that perhaps, what we are seeing isn't temperament per se, but the intensity of their temperamental traits.

"It's not your child's temper- it's your child's temperament!"
-Kytka Hilmar-Jezek

CHAPTER 5

Playing with fire

Risk Taking in Early Childhood

THEME TABLE AT A PRESCHOOL. All the objects represent the season of winter. A matchbox lies on the table, easily accessible to the children.

In South Africa, we visited a couple of preschools in northern Kruger, and were astounded by some of the things that we saw. Like boxes of matches in classrooms of 40-50 children including three infants; tiny pieces of wood, rubber and plastic that would pose choking hazards to small children; even play equipment that was missing a couple of climbing rungs.

And yet, the children maneuvered themselves around these objects with great ease. In the two-hour time frame that we were there, *not one* child touched the easy-to-access box of matches. It made me start thinking. Were we primed as individuals to be careful of certain articles, objects or animals deemed dangerous in our culture?

I remember growing up in India and reading Jataka Tales and the Panchatantra. These were stories that today's western society would be horrified to read. Presented in comic book form, they were tales of animals and morals. They usually ended with one animal killing another. The pictures were graphic – there was blood and gore. And I read them avidly!

Panchatantra, published in Sanskrit, in India, are perhaps the oldest children's stories in the world, written over 2,500 years ago. The author, Vishnu Sharma, used animal characters to convey certain morals. These stories are a real guide for parents even today to help them raise their children.

In an article, David Boudinot, librarian at the University of Victoria says,[29] "The use of fear and violence in folk and fairy tales is a contentious issue which illuminates disparities of societal difference between those firmly entrenched in beliefs of righteousness and others who believe no harm is done by frightening children with folklore." "Some people," he adds, "believe that children need to be shielded from all displays of violence, especially violence found in video games, television, and folk tales, because children might emulate it and bring harm to themselves or others."

In his opinion, the studies trying to prove that displays of violence in print and visual culture lead to fear and violence in our youth are frequently inconclusive at best, and these studies are often funded by those whose ideologies detest any mention of potentially sinful activities. Conversely, he stresses, "…there is some supportive evidence from educators and sociologists which shows fear and violence in folk tales contributing to a safer and more educated society." According to him, "Teaching fear through fairy tales is a proven method of helping children learn about safety and it can help improve a child's judgment and critical thinking skills."

I once read this quote (and just found out that it is attributed to Einstein): "A ship is always safe at the shore – but that is not what it is built for." It makes me wonder: how safe should we make preschools? Is the degree of safety culturally different? Are our children being raised to be non-risk takers? Do we surround them with a bit too much of yellow caution tape? Child development expert Betty Jones wrote an incredible article where she highlighted the fact that we need to make preschools "...as safe as needed, and not as safe as possible."[30]

According to Betty Jones, today's parents 'bubble wrap' children to keep them safe from dangers in society and the environment. In her opinion, these parents are actually depriving their children of having authentic opportunities to practice safe, planned risks. Risks that will help them grow into responsible and sensible decision makers tomorrow.

Susie Mesure, in her article, '*When we stop children taking risks, do we stunt their emotional growth?*' refers to the current culture as "the so-called compensation culture." She says, "We're trying to put adventurous play into public parks and schools but we're battling against a 'sue, sue, sue' mentality." In the same article, John O'Driscoll says "Some kids are growing up in nurseries with bouncy floors, growing up without the concept of gravel or grass. Everything they've played on bounces, which gives them a false sense of security."[31]

During my work in South Africa, I also pondered the issue of risk-taking in early childhood. The children here seem to be doing fine, even in the presence of what the western world would consider great risks. (Of course, there is statistical evidence to show that children are harmed when taking such risks, and the amount of risk, when mitigated, does make for a safer environment.)

Betty Jones' words come back to me. "Risk is inevitable; it's a requirement for survival. The challenge is to name it, practice it, enjoy the rush of mastery and bear the pain when pain is the outcome. A child who climbs may fall. But a child who never climbs is at much greater risk."[32]

"Life is either a daring adventure or nothing at all."
-Helen Keller

CHAPTER 6

"I think I can, I know I can..."

Active Learning in Early Childhood

As an educator, I learn best through direct observation: visiting preschools across countries and across cultures opens my eyes to the varied practices and pedagogies that others may have or follow. Some of the schools I spent time at in South Africa had a lot of toys; and then there were some, where the children had only a few. What surprised me, however, was the lack of engagement, not the lack of toys. I walked into classrooms where there were at least 50 children, all of whom were standing around. They stared at each other. They hardly spoke. I thought at first it was because they just saw a bunch of strangers walk in.

In the middle of the crowd of children, I saw a few children trying to engage with some toys. The rest of them just stood around.

So I stayed in the classroom. I sat on the floor and watched. A few of them came and plonked themselves on my lap. I tried to play with them. And that's when I began to realize that these children needed to learn to engage: engage with people; engage with toys; and engage with manipulatives, i.e., small toys, cars or blocks that young children can manipulate with their hands.

Friedrich Froebel, the father of Kindergarten, who, in 1837, started the world's first kindergarten program, developed different types of objects (known as "gifts") to help his kindergartners recognize patterns and appreciate geometric forms found in nature.[33] In the early 1900s, Maria Montessori further advanced the idea that manipulatives (or "materials" as they are referred to in a Montessori environment) are important in education.[34] She designed many materials to help preschool and elementary school students discover and learn basic ideas in math and other subjects. Since the early 1900s, manipulatives have come to be considered essential in teaching mathematics at not just the preschool level, but also at the elementary-school level.

Classroom management isn't just about ratios and square footage; isn't just about physical supervision. It's about teacher-child interactions and engagement. When I observed the children at play, Howard Gardner's 'Frames of Mind 'came to my mind. Gardner is an American developmental psychologist at the Harvard Graduate School of Education at Harvard University. He developed the Theory of Multiple Intelligences in 1983. What I saw before me was a myriad of intelligences: kinesthetic, logical-mathematical, spatial, interpersonal, intrapersonal, musical, linguistic. So many intelligences in one classroom. What was lacking was the most important piece: teacher engagement to help the intelligences flourish in the classroom.

Dr. Thomas Armstrong, an expert in the Theory of Multiple Intelligences, wrote, "The theory... suggests that the traditional notion of intelligence, based on I.Q. testing, is far too limited."[35] Instead, Dr. Gardner proposes eight different intelligences to account for a broader range of human potential in children and adults. These intelligences are:

- Linguistic intelligence ('word smart')
- Logical-mathematical intelligence ('number / reasoning smart')
- Spatial intelligence ('picture smart')
- Bodily-Kinesthetic intelligence ('body smart')
- Musical intelligence ('music smart')
- Interpersonal intelligence ('people smart')
- Intrapersonal intelligence ('self smart')
- Naturalist intelligence ('nature smart')

With this in mind, we started thinking of other manipulatives to make. In the span of just one evening, Todd and I created and put together bought materials for the children to manipulate. Todd made some very interesting looking cars using washers and blocks of wood, while I created some 'story boards' for the children to use. Since there was such a lack of toys and books in the local languages about the culture and lives of the children in villages, I decided to make a storyboard – a board that made child-created stories come alive. I took small planks of wood, and created mini sceneries on them: I glued fabric onto them to resemble water or land; I glued trees, plants etc. to create landscapes. Then I provided children with a basket of small toys that they could manipulate to tell their own stories. I was lucky to find small plastic crocodiles in a store- they provided endless hours of boisterous fun play!

Barbara Baker, author of '*Manipulatives: Tools for Active Learning*' states that research shows that playing with manipulatives gives children opportunities to learn about physical science. "There is so much to be gained for both children and adults from putting a strong focus on physical science in the curriculum. Children gain experience in problem solving, creative thinking, spatial relations, decision making, observation, sorting, categorizing, estimating- all essential skills for later success in science."[36]

So, let them play: As research shows, the more they play, the more they learn!

"We don't stop playing because we grow old; we grow old because we stop playing."
- George Bernard Shaw

CHAPTER 7

"You said you'd play with me. You're a liar. No I'm not a liar. I forgot. Don't call me a liar."

The Power of Imagination and Fantastic Thinking

'LYING' IS COMMON IN CHILDREN between 3 and 5. Preschoolers don't often understand that it's not right to lie, and they love to use their imaginations to make up stories. The lies that they tell are mostly harmless, and more due to their very active imaginations than anything else. Preschool lying can be divided into three categories: Children who typically tell tall tales, children who have what is referred to as the preschool 'memory lapse', and the 'seekers', children who lie because they seek out friendships.

Why do children lie and what can we do about it?

According to the advice given by the Raising Children Network, children tell lies for many reasons, depending on the situation and their motivation.[37]

Children might lie to:

- cover something up, hoping to avoid consequences or punishment.
- explore and experiment with their parents' responses and reactions.
- exaggerate a story or impress others.
- gain attention, even when they're aware the listener knows the truth.
- manipulate a situation or set something up.

Children tell different types of lies:[38]

The tall tale tellers – According to authors Kristin Zolten and Nicholas Long[39] in their article on lying, "[Preschool children]… have vivid imaginations, and are just learning to know the difference between fantasy and reality, often not differentiating between the two."[40] They state that when children tell tall tales and exaggerate, they're often expressing things that they wish were true; or they might make up something that isn't true or greatly exaggerate something that did happen. When things get broken or spilled, they are seldom the culprits – it's usually an imaginary someone else who is the perpetrator of the crime: "I didn't do it. My friend, Sammy did it."

This kind of imaginative play that sometimes results in the creation of tall tales is very common in early childhood. According to Marjorie Taylor, Professor Emeritus at the University of Oregon, "By age seven, about 37% of children take imaginative play a step further and create an invisible friend." She adds that most young children play pretend games and interact with their stuffed animals, dolls, or other special toys as if they were alive. Taylor and her colleagues found that children vividly experience interactions with their invisible friends, but they almost always know that these friends aren't real. They found that "…77% of these children said "yes" when asked if they had a pretend friend, and 40% spontaneously remarked at some point during the interview that they were talking about a pretend friend. The children offered statements such as, "Her is a fake animal," or "I just made him up in my head," and "He's not in real life." Only one child was adamant that her invisible friend was real."[41]

Lies by omission and 'Sticky Fingers'– Often, children come home with toys in their backpacks or something in their pockets. When questioned about it, their responses might be, "I don't know how it reached there." Many parents get upset because they think that their children have begun to steal. This, however, is not stealing; it can best be described as a memory lapse. As Dana Asher puts it in her article, for a preschooler, '*What's mine is mine, and what's yours is mine too,*' "Five- and 6-year-olds are in the process of developing a conscience, but it can still be very hard for them to control their impulses when they see something they want. Although they know the rules intellectually, they haven't internalized them yet."[42]

The seekers – The next category of 'liars' is the seeker: they steal to fit in with their peers. They might steal to get the cool toy, or take something because it makes them part of a particular group. They often manipulate adults into getting their way. Again, this kind of lying isn't the 'serious' lying that happens when children grow older. "They look around, see what other kids have, and feel bad if they don't have the same things," says Meri Wallace, author of the book, '*Birth Order Blues.*' In her opinion, 5- and 6-year-olds are also likely to be influenced by media and television commercials that show the trendiest toys. "Stealing, [then,] may seem like an easy way to keep up with the cool kids."[43]

What can we do about preschool lying? Peggy Drexler, in her article on lying states, "It's important to raise children to value honesty, and to prevent lying from becoming frequent and consistent, the point at which lying is most troublesome. The first step in figuring out how to address a lie is to consider why your child is telling it."[44]

It's critical to ask more, and to accuse less. Value a child's honesty; in turn children will value honesty too.

When in doubt, especially when a preschooler lies, remember these words by author Melinda Wenner Moyer, "When kids lie, it's not a sign that they're on the road to delinquency—it's a sign that they are developing important psychological skills."[45]

"A little inaccuracy sometimes saves tons of explanation."

-Saki

CHAPTER 8

"I am Captain America. When I am a superhero, I can run really fast and I can shoot fire."

Superhero Play

IT'S OUR PRIVILEGE AS EDUCATORS of young children to listen in on their thoughts, conversations and stories. Here are excerpts from conversations overheard in the play yard:

Conversation #1: between 4-year-olds
Child: *We made a trap. He's in jail. He can't get out.*
Teacher: *How do people get treated when they are in jail?*
Child: *They can't see their families and they are not allowed to leave.*
Conversation # 2: between 4 boys, aged 3-4 years old
Can I help you with your work?
Sure, Superman!
I want to be Iron Man. He is strong and can shoot fire.
I am Captain America. When I am a superhero, I can run really fast.
I want to be Batman. He has Bat Weapons to save people.

Conversations like these are heard more and more often as we approach Halloween in the United States. In India, these conversations often surface with the release of the newest action film, one that is targeted at young children. Young children engage in superhero play, run around wildly, brandishing weapons (which, if confronted by an adult, magically turn into peaceful instruments!)

60

Magic capes or tiaras transform young children into mighty superheroes; yet, we try and strip them of that very power that they are trying so hard to attain. It's uncomfortable to talk to children about violence; yet, it's imperative. To ban superhero play, or not to ban? That is the question…and the dilemma that teachers often find themselves in.

Diane Levin, child development expert, states that most young children look for ways to feel potent and strong. In her opinion, play can be a safe way to achieve a sense of power. "From a child's point of view, play with violence is very seductive, especially when connected to the power and invincibility portrayed in [media] entertainment. The children who use war play to help them feel powerful and safe are the children who feel the most powerless and vulnerable."[46]

Many educators prefer to ban games that turn violent or simulate war. Weapons are banned in classrooms. Children wear scary costumes, or superhero clothing but must leave the weapons behind during Halloween. The reality, however, is that banning rough and tumble games or superhero play rarely works. Children will find other ways to play the same games. They will hide and surreptitiously play them, away from the eyes and ears of the adult. The reason to keep this kind of play, and in fact to encourage it, is that through rough and tumble play, children are able to work out their issues and also 'slay their dragons.'

Rough and tumble play has its rightful place in the preschool classroom. To the untrained adult, this kind of play looks very much like fighting and aggression, and so, more often than not, this play comes to an abrupt stop with consequences for the children involved. Frances Carlson, author and early childhood educator, in her article on rough and tumble play, states, "Many people fear that play-fighting or rough and tumble play is the same as real fighting. There is also a fear that this rough play will become real fighting if allowed to continue. Most of all, though, parents and teachers fear that during the course of rough and tumble play a child may be hurt."[47] The reality is that this kind of play has great benefits for preschoolers. Through this play, children develop their large motor muscles that help in their full-body development.

There was one year in which I had seventeen boys in my class. Within minutes of coming in to school, the boys would invariably land on top of each other in a kind of play wrestling, something one can commonly see in the animal world when young puppies and kittens play and cavort with each other. I ordered a wrestling mat for the children, and soon we had our very own wrestling bouts. The rules were simple:

1. A teacher must be present.
2. No more than two children can wrestle at a time.
3. When a child says "no", the game stops.
4. And, no hands around a child's neck EVER.

Before we knew it, we realized that we had in fact channelized the high energy and the need for body contact that the young boys craved and needed, into something that was fun.

According to Frances Carlson, "Through the (very) physical interactions required in rough and tumble play, children are learning the give-and-take of appropriate social interactions." In her opinion, this kind of play encourages children to understand crucial non-verbal and verbal cues from other children, and also encourages a cooperative "give and take" play. She states, "… the social roles practiced and learned in rough and tumble play provide children with the social knowledge needed for future relationships."

"A little nonsense now and then is cherished by the wisest men."
-Roald Dahl

CHAPTER 9

"The world has to be protected from bad guys, guns, and killing..."

Why Bad Guys are Part of Imaginative Play

FROM THE MOUTHS OF BABES:

Child 1: *We are knights. We protect the whole world.*
Teacher: *Who does the world have to be protected from?*
Child 1: *The world has to be protected from bad guys, guns and killing.*
Child 2: *And Taser guns, earthquakes...and even tornadoes.*
Child 3: *We need to protect the world from pirates and rifles...and also not having x-rays.*
Child 4: *Too many people cut down plants and they pick flowers.*
Child 5: *Yes. People say bad words and pretend to have weapons.*
Child 6: *And people have to be protected from pinching.*

Today's world is a scary world for young children to grow up in. I still remember working with a group of young children when 9/11 happened. For months after the incident, TV and news channels replayed footage of the plane hitting one of the Twin Towers. The television shows were full of images and videos that were very frightening.

I was a young schoolgirl when Indira Gandhi was assassinated in India: again, what I remember so vividly is

63

the dramatization on TV of the shooters. This kind of visual information can be very traumatic for young children to process: to help with this, young children often engage in some form of socio-dramatic play. The author of the book *'Children understand the World Through Play'*[48] states that this play also offers young children a way to make sense of, and integrate confusing and overwhelming emotional experiences. In the preschool classroom, I have often watched as children replayed and re-enacted this terrifying scenario to assimilate that experience and also to feel less threatened or frightened by it. I have watched children build block replicas of the Twin Towers, and observed as they crashed their plastic toy airplanes into it. It's scary, overwhelming, and anxiety provoking; however, through this play, the children are better able to make sense of the trauma that they might have witnessed.

On another occasion, in another one of the classrooms, I watched children playing with plastic animals – there were rocks and wood to provide the story backdrop to support their play. The children were making sounds and matching their actions to mimic rocks falling on the animals. They said, "The animals are bad. They kill." As I spoke to them, they said, "The animals are bad because they eat meat. They are carnivores." Further discussions led to this: "The animals are bad because they kill." The killing theme seemed to be a common one for the children that day.

Children also need opportunities for large body play to help process their fears and insecurities. The curriculum in an early child environment should be structured in a manner that is conducive to large body play.

The more opportunities that children have for engaging in large physical play, the more engaged they get in the curriculum. It gives children a different outlet to help them process their fears and insecurities. Based on this observation, on one occasion, we decided to set up the environment to combine the children's need for large physical play, an outlet for their aggression and their interest in painting.

So we extended a Jackson-Pollock-like splatter painting activity and had them throw paint balls at the easel. And then, we set up a 'bounce paint' activity where half the children were the 'catchers' – standing at the edge of the paper, while the other half were the 'pitchers' – bouncing paint-soaked balls from the top of the table on to paper.

Margaret King & Dan Gartell in their article in Young Children, '*Building an Encouraging Classroom with Boys in Mind*',[49] advise us to "Respect this period as an opportunity to learn what their bodies can do." They state that children tend to get more lower body exercise than upper. "Climbing, building with various materials, and gardening develop the arms, shoulders, and trunk muscles."

Physical activity is necessary for all children, but it is especially important for young boys who enjoy running, jumping, and moving their bodies. According to Deborah F. Perry *et al* in their article, '*Expulsion From Child Care*',[50] The prevalence rates for challenging behavior in preschool classrooms, "ranges from 10% to 30%. Campbell estimated that approximately 10–15% of all typically developing preschool children have chronic mild to moderate levels of behavior problems." According to Perry *et al*,[51] "Emotional and behavioral problems of children are typically divided into two general categories: externalizing and internalizing problems. Externalizing problems involve aggressive, defiant, and noncompliant behaviors." It is this kind of behavior that teachers can help mitigate by providing a "Big-Body" environment. Not only does big body play and superhero play help children address their fears in a developmentally appropriate manner, it also helps to address behavior problems that might arise in the preschool environment.

"You may say I'm a dreamer, but I'm not the only one. I hope someday you'll join us. And the world will live as one."
-John Lennon

CHAPTER 10

"When people die, that means their battery stops working."

A Preschooler's Understanding of Death and the Importance of Inter-generational Relationships

PRESCHOOL CHILDREN ARE OFTEN BOTH fascinated and puzzled by old age and death. On one such occasion, we read the book, '*Wilfrid Gordon, McDonald Partridge*', a story by Mem Fox[52] that explores a young boy's understanding of old age and the loss of memory.

Overheard at circle time:

Child 1: *When people die, their battery stops working.*

Teacher: *When does that happen?*

Child 1: *When you are old.*

Child 2: *You could get sick or hurt to die.*

Child 1: *There's pipes in your brain. When they aren't connected, that's because you're old. That's when you're dead.*

Child 3: *You could die any time.*

Child 4: *My cats are going to die before my family because they're really little.*

Child 5: *My cat already died.*

Child 6: *You can die by a bullet from a police gun.*

Child 2: *When you die, your lungs don't work anymore. If you can't breathe, you die.*

Child 7: *You can die if someone kills you with a sword.*

Child 8: *You can die if you put your finger in a piranha's mouth.*

Child 9: *You can die at any age whenever some hockey players die. They could die if they get tired playing.*
Child 10: *You could die if you get hurt by a hockey stick.*

A child's understanding of death depends on many factors, the most important of which are the child's own experience and the developmental stage of the child. James A. Graham in his article, '*How Do Children Comprehend the Concept of Death?*' states, "Children's experiences with death (i.e., actual experience and what they have been told about death) are critical to their understanding of it."[53] He adds that children do not have enough life experience to realize that death is inevitable for all living things.

Young children do not have an understanding of concepts surrounding the topic of death. They are not always developmentally ready to understand that:

Concept 1: Death Is Irreversible: Unlike the characters in cartoons who spring back to life, when people die, they do not come back.

Concept 2: All Life Functions End Completely at the Time of Death: Children do not always understand that when people die, their body functions stop completely. David Schonfeld & Marcia Quackenbush, authors of '*After a Loved One Dies—How Children Grieve*',[54] caution parents against saying things like, "my car died." When children see the car running efficiently after a visit to the mechanic, they might assume that people too can come back to life after death.

Concept 3: Everything That Is Alive Eventually Dies: Schonfeld & Quackenbush state that "parents often reassure children that they will always be there to take care of them. They tell them not to worry about dying themselves. This wish to shield children from death is understandable, but when a death directly affects a child, this reality can no longer be hidden."

Concept 4: Death Is Caused by Physical Reasons: It's important to let children know if and when they ask how a person died. Say the authors, "If children do not understand the real reason their family member has died, they are more likely to come up with explanations that cause guilt or shame."

Conversations on topics such as death happen in classrooms, in the play yard, even in a children's bathroom. Here's another conversation about death that some children had in the sandbox:

The children were really excited to play with the dinosaurs. I watched as they took shovels and created giant mounds of sand. "Look!" they cried out to me. "We are making a volcano for our dinosaurs."

So, we got them two bags of dinosaurs to play with. Then one of the children picked up a shovel, and began to put some sand on one of the dinosaurs. She said, "The dinosaur has died. So now we have to cover the dinosaur up. No one should see it. Let's cover it till it has gone." All of the children picked up shovels and began to bury the dinosaur in the sandbox.

Overheard:
They go up in the air when they die.
You leave the earth and die.
When you die, you lose power and don't have energy to be working.
My grandfather's mom died.
When people die, you have to try and wake them up.
I buried the dinosaur to make it comfortable.
You can't come back if you die.
The dinosaurs will be comfortable if they are dead.

It's always confusing to understand how to handle conversations about death. How much do you tell a child? What do they understand? In another article on the same subject, the authors write,[55] "Their [preschoolers'] misconception [about death] is reinforced by cartoons in which characters pop back to life moments after anvils drop on them from the sky." The authors add that because young children are concrete thinkers, seeing things exactly as they appear and hearing things literally, it is important that they are told about death in simple, clear language. They advise parents and educators to not use euphemisms like, "She has gone to sleep," "…traveled to the great beyond," or "…passed away." These phrases will not be understood and may even generate fears of sleeping or taking long trips." Instead, they stress that "…young children should be told that their loved one has died and "that means we will no longer be able to see her."

It is also important to understand that children do not understand metaphorical thinking: Adults use this phrase so often to describe that their phone or laptop has run out of battery: "My phone died!" It is through meaningful conversations that young children are able to make sense of complex topics such as these.

It is crucial that young children create and have bonds with the seniors in their family. Not only are there enormous benefits to this intergenerational relationship, it also allows children to understand the process of aging and death in a developmentally appropriate way.

In today's world, there are fewer and fewer joint/blended families and far more nuclear families. With job migration, children often grow up thousands of miles from their grandparents, and as a result, they see fewer and fewer caring adults and for much shorter periods. Research shows children need four to six involved, caring adults in their lives to fully develop emotionally and socially. While peer involvement is great, and something parents strive to provide for their children, children often get too much peer socialization. This situation is compounded by the fact that they also have too much mediated contact through computers and texting, and not enough one-on-one, personal time with mature adults.

When my son was four, he often missed school to curl up on his grandmother's lap to watch a one-day cricket match. Those kinds of moments and memories are precious and cannot be replaced by academic coaching. Through grandparents and other seniors, children have a better sense of who they are and where they've come from, in terms of culture and roots. According to author, Susan V. Bosak,[56] this relationship helps children have roots, a history, and a sense of continuity and perspective.

She adds that this kind of intergenerational relationship helps children develop higher self-esteem, better emotional and social skills (including an ability to withstand peer pressure), and even have better grades in school. Many adults think that it's wrong to spoil children. 'Spoiling', as a word, is an adult connotation: spoiling, Bosak states, "is nothing but unconditional love," and it rightfully belongs in the lives of young children.

Besides being good for the child, in today's world, more than ever before, knowing older people and spending time with them, helps children challenge ageist stereotypes.

As Bosak states, it is ironic that in those at either end of the life course – the young and the old – you find striking similarities. She elaborates that we live in a society that values adulthood, and in turn 'doing' – productivity and ongoing activity. "The young and the old, [on the other hand,] share a different rhythm." It is one, she states, that focuses not only on doing, but on the power of being. "It's the simplicity of playing with blocks or tending to flowers. The young and the old are most closely connected with the essence of living!"[57]

Said the little boy, "Sometimes I drop my spoon." Said the old man, "I do that too."
The little boy whispered, "I wet my pants." I do that too," laughed the little old man.
Said the little boy, "I often cry." The old man nodded, "So do I."
But worst of all," said the boy, "it seems Grown-ups don't pay attention to me."
And he felt the warmth of a wrinkled old hand. I know what you mean," said the little old man.

-Shel Silverstein, *The Little Boy and the Old Man*

CHAPTER 11

Poop Soup and Other Tales

Potty Talk in Early Childhood

ONE DAY, I SPENT SOME time with the children in the sandbox. The children were immersed in a host of sand activities: cooking, pouring, mixing and stirring.

As I sat down to watch a group of children play, I was offered a generous helping of what was described as 'poop soup'. "Would you like to eat some soup?" "Today, we have poop soup."

Having worked with children for a huge part of my life, I am unfazed by the things said by children. When looked at from the lens of child development, even this 'poop talk' falls in the realm of ages and stages of development.

When children are young, they are working on building their vocabulary. They repeat words and practice them till they get the words and the meanings. It's important to remember that when children are either in the process of being potty trained or if they have just been potty trained, they have been exposed to the words, 'poop' and 'pee' (or any other word that you might use in your family to describe these body functions.)

They tend to use these words often because they're familiar, and because they realize that these words have the power to make their friends laugh! Lisa Medoff, in her article on potty words has this to say: "Repeating bad words (and laughing hysterically about them) is often merely a stage that most preschool and kindergarten children go through."[58]

She cautions parents to remember that words only have power and meaning because we give them power and meaning. She states that preschool children have no idea that they have said a 'bad' word until they see an adult's reaction, as they do not really understand that words can be good or bad until they are taught so by adults.

This kind of potty talk happens often in a preschool environment. A few years ago, when the children I was teaching learned that I was going to India for the holidays, they had many questions for me: "How long does it take?" "Do you have a mother?" and, of course, "Have you ever ridden on an elephant?" The third question had me thinking back to a winter in 1998, when I had visited the south Indian forest of Mudumalai, where I spent a rather uncomfortable two hours on the back of an elephant. I responded to the children, that indeed, I had ridden on an elephant, and that it wasn't comfortable. Then they had more questions for me, and somewhere along the way, we began talking about elephant poop. The conversation now took on a new turn and the children began to wonder how far the poop would have to travel in order to reach the ground when an elephant pooped—a class in physics!

Because of the intense curiosity of my students, I brought back the closest thing to elephant poop that I hygienically could – paper balls made of elephant dung paper – and showed them to the children. They were delighted and fascinated. Then I saw one of the children surreptitiously insert the paper 'dung' into an elephant puppet in order to make the elephant poop! I began to wonder about the fascination that preschoolers have with 'potty words' and why it is important in their development.

Parents often get embarrassed by their children's sense of humor especially when children seem to repeat words or phrases that they think are 'potty words'. I remember many children who seemed to almost be hooked on saying, "you're a poopy head," and each time the children said it, I remember them going into paroxysms of laughter! Many parents can't wait for their children to outgrow this stage – it's embarrassing, especially in public. We all know that kids do say the "darndest things," and in the worst of public places. It's however really important to know that this potty stage is just a stage, one that children will soon outgrow.

Michele Borba, Ed.D, author of '*The Big Book of Parenting Solutions: 101 Answers to Your Everyday Challenges and Wildest Worries*' states that "Kids this age have a budding sense of humor, and they know they'll get a response from potty language."[59] It's important to avoid overreacting to a preschooler's attempt at humor. If children don't get a reaction from you, potty talk will lose much of its appeal.

Sarah L. Smidl, in her article, '*My Daddy Wears Plucky Ducky Underwear*' stresses the role of humor in a preschooler's life. She states that it is in fact "...in this preschool period when children discover that they are in a physical body, the body belongs to them, and their body can do weird things and make peculiar noises."[60]

The American Academy of Pediatrics highlights the fact that the use of 'toilet words' and toilet training go hand in hand; thus, it not uncommon to see young preschoolers going through a phase of using potty words. "Bathroom humor, or potty talk, commonly accompanies toilet training and preschool development in general. Three-and four-year-olds become interested in these words as they hear them increasingly from you during toilet training or from their friends during play."[61] It is important for parents (and preschool educators) to set clear limits on what's not acceptable, and give children a reason. It's important to balance those limits with a clear message that a child's body and its functions are nothing to be ashamed of. It's also important to remember that between 18 and 36 months, children begin toilet training and learn the language for genitals and body functions from their family and teachers in the home language the child uses. Both caregivers and families should use accurate names for body parts (although many feel uncomfortable about doing so) and letting children know, without embarrassment, that bodily functions (like poop or pee, susu or potty) are a natural part of everyone's life.

Sarah L. Smidl urges us to remember that "the laughter that results from "having the body involved" in experiential learning further supports the importance of continuing to include these opportunities not only in early childhood education, but throughout life."

"Your children are not your children. They are the sons and daughters of Life's longing for itself...
You may house their bodies but not their souls, for their souls dwell in the house of tomorrow, which you cannot visit, not even in your dreams."

-Khalil Gibran

CHAPTER 12

"Sometimes you can have two dads and sometimes you can have two moms. And some day, my parents will get married."

Questioning Ideas and Challenging Bias

OFTEN, I HAVE LISTENED TO children have deep discussions about topics that are surprisingly adult:

Who is God?

Have you ever seen God?

What does it mean to be married?

On one such day, the children were engaged in a serious conversation of what it meant to be married. The following is an excerpt of the conversation that some four-year-olds had:

Child1: *You can't have a son if you are not married.*

Child 2: *That's not true. My babysitter has a baby and she only has a boyfriend.*

Child 3: *Yes. And sometimes you can have two dads and sometimes you can have two moms. And some day, my parents will get married.*

Child 2: *You can marry her (points to girl sitting opposite him.)*

(Teacher: *So, what does marry mean?)*

Child 3: *It means "You kiss somebody."*

Child 1: *And also the boy asks the girl, "Will you marry me?"*

Child 4: *Marry means getting engaged.*

Child 5: *The guy that's marrying you, he's your husband.*
Child 6: *Marry means you kiss someone, they hug and they love each other.*
Child 3: *And the girls wear dresses.*
Child 7: *And you can marry an animal. And animals can marry a baby animal. And I am going to marry an ambulance.*
Child 3: *You can't marry an ambulance.*
Child 2: *Yes. Only people can marry people.*
(**Teacher**: *Do you know that certain groups of people in India and in a place called Nepal marry trees. What do you think about that?*)
Child 7: *Then I think I will marry an ambulance.*

Why are such conversations important both at home and in a preschool environment? Children need to have such conversations, question their beliefs (and ours) to make better sense of the world that they live in. For most young children, the preschool environment is the first social environment where they meet and play with children of their own age. As children develop, they learn to see the differences and similarities in people. I still remember walking behind a pregnant woman in Mumbai with my then two-year-old son. In a loud stage whisper (that everyone could hear) he asked, "Mama, why is she so fat?" I cringed with embarrassment when he uttered those words, as do so many other parents.

Now, many years later, I realize that those were the years for him to learn and understand anti- bias, and for him to learn how to get along with other children. Children see similarities; children also notice differences. This is the reason why children need adults to have meaningful conversations with them.

According to Louise Derman-Sparks & Julie Olson Edwards,[62] "Anti-bias education is needed because children live in a world that is not yet a place where all of them have equal opportunity to become all they could be. We know children need to feel safe and secure in all their many identities, feel pride in their families, and feel at home in their early childhood programs. We also know that children need tools to navigate the complex issues of identity, diversity, prejudice, and power in their daily lives so that they may learn, thrive, and succeed." Derman-Sparks and Edwards state that how children expect to be treated and how they treat others is significantly shaped in the early childhood setting. "In developmentally appropriate practice, practitioners create and foster a 'community of learners' that supports all children to develop and learn."

The vision that early child educators have of anti-bias education is as follows. In this world:
"All children and families have a sense of belonging and experience affirmation of their identities and cultural ways of being.
All children have access to and participate in the education they need, to become successful, contributing members of society.
The educational process engages all members of the program or school in joyful learning.
Children and adults know how to respectfully and easily live, learn, and work together in diverse and inclusive environments.
All families have the resources they need to fully nurture their children.
All children and families live in safe, peaceful, healthy, comfortable housing and neighborhoods." [63]

It is imperative that classrooms of today strive to set up environments where all children feel safe. In preschool classrooms especially, it is important to raise issues that challenge the status quo, that help children understand right and wrong. By scaffolding their conversations, teachers help children become independent thinkers who will learn to stand up against bullies and bias in later life. It is in fact this kind of conversation that will grow more Rosa Parks, more Nelson Mandelas, more Mahatma Gandhis and more Martin Luther Kings.

"You may say I'm a dreamer, But I'm not the only one
I hope someday you'll join us, And the world will live as one"
                                                  -John Lennon, *Imagine*

CHAPTER 13

"That's mine!"

Understanding Egocentric Thinking in Early Childhood

THERE IS ALWAYS A LOT of "That's mine!" in preschool classrooms. The toys, the water, and yes, even the sand is 'mine'. This kind of behavior is very typical in a toddler or preschool classroom as young children learn to form relationships with their peers. In fact, 3- and 4-year-olds tend to cling passionately to their possessions. "Preschoolers are so focused on their own wants and needs that sharing just isn't a priority,"[64] explains Ann Easterbrooks, Ph.D., chair of the Eliot-Pearson Department of Child Development at Tufts University, in Medford, Massachusetts.

As educators, we pay a lot of attention to fostering this kind of pro-social relationship in children. According to Grayden Gordon on the Sesame Street website, "pro-social behavior is when children show positive behaviors such as sharing, cooperating, empathy, and taking turns when interacting with others. These skills can help children build strong friendships and relationships and enable children to navigate different social circumstances in a constructive manner."[65]

We want children to care and share and show empathy. According to authors Marilou Hyson and Jackie L. Taylor,[66] starting early is important, because early pro-social tendencies often continue into later years. In a study, it was found that "Children who are more pro-social when they begin school continue to be more pro-social in the primary grades…: one study that followed children from preschool into early adulthood found that children who were observed to spontaneously share toys more often than their classmates showed more pro-social skill 19 years later."

While educators encourage young children to share, others feel that sharing is not developmentally appropriate for every age: very young children don't always have the ability to share. There are some who believe in the idea that children must share everything; and others who will equip an environment with multiples of toys just so that there is no conflict. Some even advocate a no- sharing policy.

Becky Worley, in an ABC News article, looked closely at this practice. "…only when a child is done playing with something can another child take the toy." Rather than focusing on the importance of sharing, Worley looks at the practice of delayed gratification with regard to toys and possessions. "The child asking for the toy learns to wait." Adults don't hurry to replicate those toys, or satisfy the child's needs. She continues, "Developmentally that skill is called delayed gratification. It teaches a child that the world is not set up to automatically and immediately meet all of their needs."[67]

As educators, we look for what we call 'teachable moments' – moments that happen every day that help us teach young children certain things that we would like them to know, learn and practice in the safety of a preschool environment. Yes, sharing is certainly one of those skills that we look for in early childhood; however, we teach children to share only when they are developmentally ready to do so.

Another skill that helps children move from their egocentric selves to a place where they can understand and appreciate the perspective of others, is conflict resolution. By providing children with many of the same toy, and by not allowing them to learn and practice delayed gratification, we take away the opportunity from children of learning to resolve conflicts in a developmentally appropriate way.

It's important to delicately balance where children are developmentally, and what skills they may be ready to master: both sharing and the concept of conflict resolution are needed to help children grow and develop to become pro-social adults in later life.

"The Rainbow Fish shared his scales left and right. And the more he gave away, the more delighted he became. When the water around him filled with glimmering scales, he at last felt at home among the other fish."
-Marcus Pfister, *The Rainbow Fish*

By assuming roles and interacting with other children
they practice language and social skills including
sharing and cooperation helping and problem solving.

Children need to have the freedom to explore
materials more freely and have more sensory
experiences and enjoy messy art fun.

Curiosity is the very basis of education.

Magic capes or tiaras transform young children into mighty superheroes.

Play is a complex occupation requiring practice in dialogue and exposition, detailed imagery literary allusion and abstract thinking.

retend play gives a child a miniature world where he or she is
e mother or the father and all of the toys manageable and easily
manipulated.

Shiny mirrors and sparkling beads and transparent fabrics and reflected light focus attention on new ways of seeing the world.

The dinosaur has died. So now we have to cover the dinosaur up. No one should see it. Let us cover it till it has gone.

The world has to be protected from bad guys guns and killing.

Empathy is learned in the preschool classroom.

The best toys are the simplest ones.

Children also need opportunities for large body play to help process their fears and insecurites.

Education is the most powerful weapon which you can use to change the world.

For children play is serious
learning. Play is really the
work of childhood.

The important thing is not to stop questioning.
Curiosity has it's own reason for questioning.

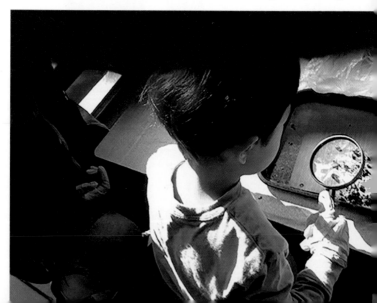

COGNITIVE DEVELOPMENT

Cognitive development refers to the development of the ability to think and reason. In young children, this occurs in different stages, as they grow from the preoperational stage to the concrete operational one.

This section is largely based on my experiences as a Teaching Fellow in South Africa. When my colleague Todd Hioki and I were on our six-week Teaching Fellowship to South Africa, we had the opportunity to observe children in their natural environments. We were fortunate to be able to spend time in their classrooms watching them learn, play and develop.

CHAPTER 1

"Free the child's potential...and you will transform him into the world."

-Maria Montessori

On the Importance of Stimulating Environments

PRESCHOOL TEACHERS SHOULD CREATE ENVIRONMENTS that invite curiosity, ones that inspire awe, ones that provide comfort, and above all, ones that invite play. We try to transform each classroom with a view to transforming a child's experience in preschool. What surprises me is how little attention the youngest in the teachers' care receive. According to statistics on the UNICEF website, around the world, 59 million primary school children are not in the classroom, and the number is growing. Across the Middle East and North Africa, some 13 million children are not in school because of conflict and war. Nearly 9,000 schools in Syria, Iraq, Yemen and Libya are not in use because they have been damaged or destroyed.[68] The youngest children, the most vulnerable, seem to be left to their own devices in environments that are bare and devoid of any stimulation whatsoever.

While teachers are eager to equip classrooms for older children (the 4s and 5s), they seem disinclined to do much for the babies and the toddlers. All resources are directed towards the older children. Many preschool classrooms around the world are in much disrepair, and the children sit on mats or chairs, literally staring into space. There's a vacant expression on their faces where there should be joy and excitement, energy and emotion. The children sit stacked against each other, (depressingly so) much as sits a deck of dominoes…and they slide up against each other when they fall asleep.

A classroom has to go way beyond fulfilling a young child's basic needs – a classroom should offer opportunities for encouraging playfulness, mystery, wonder, and awe. The classroom should have areas or 'learning centers'[69] to be curious in, materials to interact with; soft spaces to be alone in…a classroom should be so much more than just 4 walls.

Once, when I spent some time in a preschool classroom, I had the opportunity to learn a lot about creatures that live in the sea- it was all about shark tails, shark fins, and shark teeth! The children were really fascinated by sharks. They were full of shark facts! One of the children asked me: "Did you know that a shark has many teeth, many, many teeth? It has 23 teeth!" Since I had heard that they were curious about sharks, I brought in a shark jaw for them to examine. I set the jaw on the table and watched as they gingerly explored the teeth of the great shark. "It's sharp!" they exclaimed. Ruth Wilson in her article, '*Promoting the Development of Scientific Thinking*' states that in their pursuit of knowledge, children are prone to poking, pulling, tasting, pounding, shaking, and experimenting. "From birth, children want to learn and they naturally seek out problems to solve."[70]

Children in the preschool years need environments that are rich for exploration. They also need to strengthen their fine motor muscles to get their hands ready for writing. It's therefore not surprising to see a variety of manipulatives available for children to use, as children need them to work their hands. Manipulatives are tools that help enhance and strengthen a child's fine motor skills and they exist in most classrooms in the form of blocks, Legos, small cars, etc. By manipulating objects like blocks, or beads or cars, children develop better eye-hand coordination; their handedness (left or right) gets determined; and they are more prepared to hold a pencil and write in their elementary years.

In fact, manipulatives are a huge part of the preschool environment. It is through the interaction with such material that children are able to grow and develop other skills as well. "Play activities, such as cutting, eating, writing, buttoning, painting, and dressing, provide for their [children's] fine motor development, or refinement of the skills that require the use of smaller muscles. Through play, children are naturally able to use and learn to refine their gross and fine motor skills and coordination. As children get older, they use their muscles in continually more complex ways, integrating large and fine muscle movements with visual perception."[71]

Exploring their physical environment comprises a great deal of the 'curriculum' for mobile infants and toddlers. After all, curriculum is everything that happens in the day of a child: drop-offs, explorations, meals, toileting, play, and yes, early academics too. We must, therefore, consider the impact of environment on children and caregivers, and learn to design classrooms and spaces that contribute appropriately to children's development.

While we were working in South Africa, my colleague Todd and I created a kind of "Hierarchy of Needs" for teachers:

- Step 1: Equip material for the classroom (buy, make, create…).
- Step 2: Invite children to engage with the material.
- Step 3: Allow teachers to observe children at play: prompt asking of questions; clarify.
- Step 4: Mentor teachers; allow them to connect theory with practice: let them connect the dots: the what, the how and the why of lesson and curriculum planning.

Todd and I tried to work with preschool environments in South Africa. We realized that unless teachers see that given the right environment, children *will* engage with materials, teachers will not have the "a-ha" moment that we wish them to have.

So we created/bought materials that we thought were integral to a toddler classroom: blocks, colorful toys, soft toys, sensory materials, easels at toddler height, mirrors. And then, we invited the children to come in and play. What happened next brought tears to my eyes. The room was suddenly filled with very busy toddlers. There was a beautiful hum in the room, of children's voices; there was laughter. And there was play.

Why is this so important? So crucial? There is important new scientific evidence that suggests the first three years of life are much more important in the long-term development of young children than previously believed.[72]

We learn what we do. Larry Schweinhart, in the journal, '*Wisdom of Play*'[73] underlines the idea that active learning is the way we all learn. He states, "We learn from what we see, feel, touch, taste, smell, and do. We develop the special human abilities of language-speaking, listening, reading, writing, and discovering meaning. These new abilities enrich our lives with whole new realms of knowledge, but they never replace our immediate world of senses and activities." In short, "We learn what we do."

As one walks around progressive classrooms rich with materials, one gets a chance to observe children working with their hands. In one classroom, I watched as young preschoolers manipulated nuts and bolts and tried to work small machines: they used simple machines, they held cars, they opened and closed plastic eggs, and they beaded. All the children were immersed in authentic learning experiences – learning from that they were doing. Sue Miles in her article on early childhood learning[74] states that when young children are involved in exploration and discovery, they are enthusiastic and motivated. These are the constructive principles of discovery and exploration. Children gather information through their senses and make hypotheses, test predictions, and discuss results. This is how children gain knowledge.

It's not just genetics that influences brain development, but the child's environment as well. Connections that are used repeatedly during a child's early years become the foundation for the brain's organization and its function through the child's life. In contrast, a connection that is not used at all results in the lack of their development.

"The world is full of magic things, patiently waiting for our senses to grow sharper."

-W. B. Yeats

CHAPTER 2

"Hoover Tower does not fall down because it has scotch tape!"

On Building up, Building down, Building Sideways, and Building Knowledge.

WHEN I WAS A TEACHER at Stanford University, I took the children from Rainbow School, the International Preschool at Stanford University, on a field trip to the Hoover Tower. As we lay flat on our backs on the soft grass, looking up at the tower, I asked the children, "How come the tower does not fall down?" The responses to my question were so creative. "…because it has scotch tape!" and "…because it is made of Lego bricks."

Block building – or building up, building down and building out, as it happens in the preschool classroom, has played a huge role in helping build children's thinking and problem solving skills.

Block building is essential for children to learn and practice their spatial thinking. As they play with blocks, preschoolers have to decide where to place a block- over or under another block, beside one block, or build upwards by placing one block over another. They ask questions – "Why does it fall?" "How does it stay up?" "Why can't it reach the ceiling?" They hypothesize – "Because it's too heavy," "Because it has too few blocks."

They learn concepts such as balance, stability, gravity, and cause and effect. And they learn to understand and appreciate failure. Towers get built up… and ever so often, towers come crashing down. Thus, building has been as much an exercise in physics and reason, as it has been one in self-reliance, patience and persistence.

Karen Wise Lindeman and Elizabeth McKendry Anderson, in their article on blocks and manipulatives, *'Using Blocks to Develop 21st Century Skills'*[75] state: "When they play with blocks, children are actually engaging in design technology – the creation of something that is useful or helpful or that solves a problem. The discussion of form and function regarding tool use is also an important part of design technology. A tool's design, or form, is what makes it useful. By interacting with simple forms and shapes of blocks (pillars versus circular curves in wood unit blocks) as well as with various types of blocks (magnetic, interlocking, waffle), children have multiple opportunities to learn about design technology by engaging with shape, form, and function."

Blocks are truly the building blocks of knowledge. They help children develop in all of the domains of development: social, cognitive, and physical. When children engage in block play, you often hear them narrating as they build: "I'm building a rocket ship that can reach the sky," or "Look, look. Help me: I'm making a gun that shoots elephants into the sky!"

Often, we see children engaged in some kind of symbolic play, making "guns that shoot elephants into the sky," or "traps'." Authors Julie Sarama and Douglas H. Clements state that symbolic or pretend play "…engenders the growth of representation and decontextualization, [and]… is important as a child grows for understanding more sophisticated mathematical concepts, up through algebra."[76] The authors add, "In constructive play, children manipulate objects to make something. This constitutes about 40 percent of three-year-olds' play and 50 percent of the play of four- to six-year-olds. The attraction for the child lies in playing with alternate ways of building something."

A Kaleidoscope of Children

It's fascinating to watch children interact as they build. Children tend to narrate to each other what they are building: thus, block building becomes a social activity, not just a cognitive one.

- "See, I'm making a pattern: first blue, then red."
- "I made a pattern and a shape."
- "And I made the letter M."
- "My pattern is a hexagon."

I have seen children create and explore patterns, identify and make shapes, compare and build structures. The benefits of building with blocks (and manipulatives) are many. There is a lot of mathematics and physics embedded in children's play. As young children play with blocks, they explore different dimensions of mathematics:

- Classification: grouping, sorting, or categorizing by attributes.
- Magnitude: describing or comparing the size of objects.
- Enumeration: saying number words, counting, instantly recognizing a number of objects or reading or writing numerals.
- Dynamics: putting things together, taking them apart, or exploring motions such as flipping.
- Pattern and Shape: identifying or creating patterns or shapes or exploring geometric properties.
- Spatial Relations: describing or drawing a location or direction.[77]

According to Elizabeth S. Hirsch, author of the 'Block Book', "Cognitively, children learn math and science through experiences with block size, shape, and volume, and learn language through expressing their thoughts during block-building sessions."[78] Block play, in her opinion, helps in the overall development of young children in all three domains of development: physical, cognitive and social-emotional. They learn to share ideas and blocks with each other, sometimes building structures cooperatively; they hone their fine motor skills as they build with the blocks; and they understand the concepts of balance and symmetry as they build complex structures using blocks. In addition, self-regulation is required to remain part of the group. They use their small motor muscles as they balance each block on top of another and as they build either vertically or horizontally.

Sharon MacDonald, through observation of block play, has determined that as children build, they go through stages[79] (as they do in most areas of development).

- Stage One (Ages 2-3): Children explore the properties of blocks by moving, touching and holding. They seldom build 'up' but prefer to build 'out'.
- Stage Two (Age 3): The "stack and row" stage where children stack blocks vertically or lay them horizontally, repeating the same designs over and over.
- Stage Three (Ages 3-4): Children begin building structures, especially bridges.
- Stage Four (Age 4): They begin to develop problem-solving skills by making enclosed structures.
- Stage Five (Ages 5-6): Play becomes very elaborate, and symmetrical patterns begin to appear and children begin to name their structures.
- Stage 6 (Age 6): Children work cooperatively to build a common structure.

As a teacher, it's fun to add to the block area using fabric, pine cones, cars – anything that brings a different dimension to the play. More often than not, children will incorporate *all* that they can get their hands on when building their structures (and clean up becomes a nightmare!)

Block Building: Notes & reflections from an emergent project

Elizabeth Jones, the guru of emergent curriculum, describes it as "… curriculum that emerges from the play of children and the play of teachers. It is coconstructed by the children and the adults, and the environment itself. To develop curriculum in depth, adults must notice children's questions and invent ways to extend them, document what happens, and invent more questions. The process is naturally individualized."[80]

It was construction week (and month) at the preschool. We started off the year with the children constructing roads that the "dinosaurs had destroyed". We watched, we observed, and then we set up the environment to pique their interest and to follow their lead. When teachers practice an emergent curriculum, they observe the actions of young children, and then, based on their observations, they set up the environment to provoke their interest. This leads children to deeper inquiry. While setting up the environment for the construction project, we observed a keen interest in mathematical concepts through the process of the children's construction, and heard them make comments such as "My Eiffel Tower is tall."

Smita Guha, in her article for NAEYC, '*Integrating Mathematics for Young Children through Play*'[81] states that "Young children who learn number concepts and other mathematical knowledge through hands on play activities and discussions gain a broad understanding of math skills."

We saw the children poring over the architecture books that we had set out on the table. Observing that the children had a keen interest in towers, we set out building material for the children to use to create their towers. They were busy learning to use the glue gun to build the towers and fantastic machines that that they had been talking about. Through this gluing activity, the children learned about physics – concepts such as gravity, weight and balance. They also explored the properties of matter – softness and hardness.

In addition, they learned about height, length, measurement, shape, and concepts like 'same as', and 'more than, less than'. Building sculptures offered children the opportunity to learn about, explore, understand, and experiment with the idea of three-dimensional designs.

Based on our observations of the children's keen interest in both block-building and woodworking, we decided to build a structure that they were interested in. Bridges seemed to be a common theme, so we explored a book on bridges and decided to build the Golden Gate Bridge. The children looked at the basket of wood and chose pieces that they felt were best suited to the construction. One decided that corks were best for the walls and for the 'bottom' of the bridge; one chose solid pieces of pine wood to create the base and another decided that the triangle shapes of the bridge could be made using popsicle (ice cream) sticks.

A couple of days later (after many pieces of wood, many wine corks and many, many popsicle sticks had been used) their bridge was close to being ready. It still needed the finishing touches: the Golden Gate Bridge needed another coat of gold paint (to make it golden) and the black road on the bridge needed white lines in the median.

We used a four step process of investigation for our emergent plan:[82]

- Sparks (provocations): Identify emerging ideas, look at children's interests, hold conversations, provide experiences: *The ideas that emerged were about bridges.*
- Conversations: Have conversations with interested participants, ask questions, document conversations: *We documented their ideas about materials that bridges were built with, and the reason that people build bridges.*
- Opportunities and experience: Provide opportunities and experiences in both the classroom and the community for further investigation: *We took the children on a field trip to see a bridge and to understand "how it stays up."*
- More questions and more theories – think further about the process: *We built a bridge and then tested our bridge over a "flowing river" created by a water hose.*

As teachers, we relied on the principles of constructivism by encouraging children into an inquiry-based process in which they construct learning through experience, research, and working cooperatively with others. According to Barbara Sprung, "this kind of hands-on science inquiry is intrinsically constructivist." She stresses that in early childhood, this inquiry is process-oriented. "While there may ultimately be a 'right' answer, it is an answer that children arrive at through a process of discovery guided by an adult, not something they memorize and repeat by rote."[83]

Concepts and ideas explored during the construction of the bridge:

- Gravity
- Weight
- Symmetry
- Ramps
- The properties of a hot glue gun
- Size and weight of wood
- Aesthetics

Overheard:

- *We need to lower the bridge so that cars can get on it. We need to build a ramp.*
- *Let's use popsicle sticks to build the ramp.*
- *And we can cut the corks and make speed bumps on the bridge.*
- *We have to build a wall on the bridge. Otherwise the cars will fall off.*

"Matilda said, "Never do anything by halves if you want to get away with it. Be outrageous. Go the whole hog. Make sure everything you do is so completely crazy it's unbelievable..."
-Roald Dahl, *Matilda*

CHAPTER 3

"Grown-ups never understand anything by themselves, and it is tiresome for children to be always and forever explaining things to them"

-Antoine de Saint-Exupery, The Little Prince

Looking at Art in a Preschool Environment

"WHAT A BEAUTIFUL PICTURE! GREAT job!" In my three decades of working with children, this is perhaps the most dreaded of all parent comments about children's art. There is probably *nothing* more non-descriptive about a child's art than empty praise.

Ever so often, what an adult thinks a child has drawn is far from what they have really drawn. I have even heard a child say to her parent, "It's not a beautiful flower. I just scribbled for fun." It's like in Antoine de Saint-Exupery's '*The Little Prince*'. The picture the Little Prince drew was not of a hat, but of a boa constrictor swallowing an elephant. But, who would have known? One would have probably commented (as they did in the book): "What a beautiful hat."

As Alfie Kohn writes in his article,[84] children are now hooked on praise. They do anything – draw a picture, read two lines from a book...anything...and then they look at their parent askance: "Where's MY praise?" He writes, "Hang out at a playground, visit a school, or show up at a child's birthday party, and there's one phrase you can count on hearing repeatedly: "Good job!"

But are parents solely at fault? I think not. The problem is that we have drifted away from process-based art to product-based art in preschool environments. Today, when you walk into a classroom during the month of November in the US, you are sure to see lines of turkeys, resplendent with colored feathers, hanging on walls, reminding you that Thanksgiving is around the corner. Or if you walk into a classroom in India, dozens of glittering diyas (lamps) line the walls to announce the celebration of Diwali. Do little children, between 2 and 5 years old really need to create cookie-cutter art? What do they really learn from that product that they have created? How to add five feathers to the turkey? How to cut identical looking lamps? Isn't this just "coloring between the lines" for preschool children?

Art for children must be about the process, and not about the product. It's about development: development of muscles; development of ideas and imagination; development of the child. What it's not: development of a final product.

Art begins with early scribbles. Rhoda Kellogg was a psychologist and a nursery school educator. She spent many years collecting the scribbles of young children and categorized them into distinct stages of art development.[85] She found that in their artwork and scribbles, children develop placement patterns, emergent diagram shapes, diagrams, combines, aggregates, mandalas, suns, radials, before humans and early pictorialism.

The NAEYC description of process based art:[86]
There are no step-by-step instructions.
There is no sample for children to follow.
There is no right or wrong way to explore and create.
The art is focused on the experience and on   exploration of techniques, tools, and materials.
The art is unique and original.
The experience is relaxing or calming.
The art is entirely the children's own.
The art experience is a child's choice.
Ideas are not readily available online.

And what is it that we, as parents and teachers should do when children bring a piece of art to show us? We should *not* say, "That's beautiful, great job!"

Instead here's what we all can do – ask questions of the child, even if you see only scribbles. "Tell me more about your picture." Or, "I like the shapes that you have created in your picture. I see a triangle here and a circle there..." Or we can say, "I really like the way you have mixed those colors." This allows the child to describe what he or she has drawn. It might just be like the boa constrictor and the hat story; on the other hand, sometimes, it could just be a child's free expression, and the drawing may be of nothing in particular. All of this helps a child develop his skills of creating a masterpiece and grow through the process of creating that masterpiece.

We parents often tend to compliment children on what we *think* their drawing is about: "That's a great house..." or "that's a lovely fish." We also assume that trees should be green or suns yellow or skies blue. It's important to note that children learn more when we don't focus so much on what they are drawing, but on what they are thinking about their drawing. Children describe their art as they make impressions and create their pictures. I hear them choosing their colors: "I like the pink one." They describe their art: "See mama, I drew a dot. And more dots." And sometimes, there are stories that accompany their drawing: "I drew a fairy. See her wings. And I drew a house for her." But as adults, we gaze intently at children's artwork, and sometimes, just like the adults in '*The Little Prince*', we don't quite 'see' what the children see.

Adults value finished products. The finished results of a young child's work are not as important to that child as the exploration and experimentation that went into creating them. Once kids know they can explore and discover on their own, they stop worrying about how things must look. For example, a child may mix all the colors of the rainbow and make a brown smooshy painting. But think about what he saw and learned as he mixed all those colors together.

As author Khaled Hosseini said, "Children aren't coloring books. You don't get to fill them with your favorite colors."

Process-Based Art In A Preschool Classroom - A Peek into Painting in the Style of Michelangelo

(WHO IS, ACCORDING TO A three-year-old, "the guy who painted upside down on a ceiling.")

When environments are set up in an inviting and aesthetically pleasing manner, children derive a special sensory experience from their play. In all of the areas in the classroom, I use what the Reggio philosophy refers to as 'provocations'.

In the article '*Be Reggio Inspired: Learning Experiences*',[87] the author highlights the very same reasons that I use provocations in my environments: "In Reggio-inspired preschools experiences are set up by teachers with attention to aesthetics, organization, thoughtfulness, provocation, communication and interaction."

I use provocations everywhere: at the art table (works of great artists), in the dramatic play area (to extend learning and vocabulary), and in the block area (books on architecture, 3D objects).

The Provocation: What's it like to paint on a ceiling like Michelangelo did?

The Setting: Paper taped to the bottom of the table.

What Transpired: The children lay on their backs and tried to paint under the table, in the style of Michelangelo painting on the ceiling of the Sistine Chapel. It was interesting to watch them as they stretched their arms to reach the table, or as they contorted their bodies to reach a corner they wished to paint. They commented that the paint was too heavy, and that it dripped on their faces.

To piggy-back on the experience of painting under the table, we taped some paper to an inclined surface. We had objects for gluing: some light objects like feathers and pompoms; and some heavy objects like metal bottle caps and pieces of wood. The children were eager to try their hands at the activity: some were frustrated since the objects kept falling off; others patiently problem-solved, and narrated their ideas to the other children. It was indeed all about the process, and not about the product!

Overheard:

- *The glue is too drippy. Everything keeps falling off.*
- *Oh no. It falls. Things fall because there's not enough glue and it's too heavy.*
- *It won't stick. I know. It's too heavy. Well. I can try.*
- *Things fall because there's not much glue. Let's put one big glop of glue and see. Sometimes things fall and sometimes they don't. If you want to glue the bottle caps, you have to turn them over. Then they will stick.*
- *If you want something to stick then you have to press it into the glue and hold it there for some time.*

Wonderful ideas are built on other wonderful ideas. According to Eleanor Duckworth, author of 'The Having of Wonderful Ideas', "In Piaget's terms, you must reach out to the world with your own intellectual tools and grasp it, assimilate it, yourself....Schools and teachers can provide materials and questions in ways that suggest things to be done with them; and children, in the doing, cannot help being inventive."[88]

Art Appreciation and the Preschool Child

IT'S NOT OFTEN THAT YOU see a bunch of preschoolers discussing the art style of Michelangelo or that of Pollock. This makes taking young children to museums very necessary (despite how exhausting the trip might be). What can children learn from objects and paintings in museums?

According to an article in the Smithsonian, "By carefully looking at the objects they're seeing in the exhibits, children's minds become engaged, and the objects become learning tools." The author adds that this observation "...acts as a springboard for new thoughts and ideas, stimulating the use of critical thinking skills.

Some of these skills include:

- Comparing and contrasting — recognizing similarities and differences in objects.
- Identifying and classifying — recognizing and grouping things that belong together.
- Describing — giving verbal or written descriptions of the objects viewed.
- Predicting — guessing what might happen.
- Summarizing — presenting information that has been gathered in a shortened or condensed form."[89]

Art in Action in the Preschool Classroom – Questions, Questions, and More Questions

CHILDREN ARE NATURALLY CURIOUS AND ask lots of questions. Adults can have great conversations with their children not just by listening, but by asking good questions: "What do you think this is?", "What shapes do you see?", "Why does it not fall?", "What does it make you think of?"

A few years ago, the children in my preschool classroom looked at the works of Wassily Kandinsky and tried to create an interpretation of his work. We asked the children about the shapes that they saw, we talked about the colors that Kandinsky uses, and then we looked in the environment for objects that we could trace to create those shapes. The children collected cardboard tubes, strawberry baskets, wooden blocks, and rocks to create the patterns that they saw in Kandinsky's picture.

Overheard:

- *We're making circles. I see many circles in his pictures (Kandinsky's).*
- *I'm making circles inside circles.*
- *Look, I can make circles with two hands.*
- *I see many shapes.*
- *We need some squares too.*

Through this 'project' the children were able to engage in the three skills for lifelong learning: creativity, collaboration and communication. The activity was open ended: the children could choose the materials that appealed to them; there was no right or wrong way to engage in the activity; and in fact, there was no end product. The project grew each day.

Creativity, as Michael Nobleza, Executive Director, Children's Creativity Museum states, "…is indeed a cognitive skill for which all kids have a natural disposition. Children are able to explore, take risks, learn from trial and error and generate out-of-the-box ideas fairly easily compared to adults."[90]

"Others have seen what is and asked why. I have seen what could be and asked why not. "

-Pablo Picasso

CHAPTER 4

Messy art, creativity, and poverty

Finding the Right Balance

I JUST LOVE THIS QUOTE by Sydney Gurewitz Clemens: "Art has the role in education of helping children become more themselves instead of more like everyone else." She goes on to say, "Each child's inner existence calls for expression and takes pleasure in such expression. The arts can be the medium for this expression if children have access to materials, the time to explore them, and respectful encouragement in their exploration."[91]

Art is very important in a young child's life. Children need art experiences to be creative and to flourish. And yet, in many preschools around the world, few art projects would truly count as art experiences. Perhaps this is because art material is expensive, and very hard to come by. Crayons and paper are rationed out. And sometimes, all there is for a child to color with is a tiny stub of crayon and an A4 size of paper.

Children need to have freedom of movement of their whole body. They need to make sweeping movements with their entire upper bodies – shoulders, arms, forearms, hands and fingers. Small A4 sized paper doesn't really afford children these large movements.

Another reason for giving children larger sheets of paper is that young children need to work on crossing the midline.

The body midline is an imaginary line through the center of the body, running from a point at the top of the head, to a point between the two feet. The body pivots about this central core.[92] Midline crossing describes the child's ability to make effective use of his right hand in the left body space, and the left hand in the right body space. During a classroom observation in South Africa, We observed several young children who were still unable to cross the midline. Some children turned the A4 sized paper as they colored, and some turned the paper as they tried cutting with scissors.

However, what really curtails children's expression, besides a lack of resources, is the lack of space. When you have 40-60 children packed into small rooms, and where space is at a premium, the solution cannot merely be restricted to larger paper sizes.

Another aspect to think about is the presentation of art material. Preschools have containers completely crammed with pencils with the lead broken, or with little stubs of crayons. The problem that ensues is understandable: how do you encourage children to be inspired enough to create their masterpieces when the art material is not inviting, and when there really isn't enough to go around?

Yet another feature that is completely absent in many classrooms is messy art. Art experiences themselves are absent; thus asking for messy art experiences is perhaps a bit much.

Poverty should be taken into account when making observations like mine above, because it hugely impacts how and what is done in a preschool classroom. The UNICEF website states, "Education transforms lives and breaks the cycle of poverty that traps so many children. Education for girls is particularly important — an educated mother will make sure her own children go to, and stay in, school."[93] As we already know, this education should be all round education, and must include the arts.

The answer to this problem lies in just doing more, and also in appreciating what is already being done. It's easy to say that larger sheets of paper are needed or that more crayons should be bought. It's far more difficult to wonder where the money to buy those materials will come from. The journey to changing this is slow, but it will happen. Children need to have the freedom to explore materials more freely, have more sensory experiences, and enjoy messy art fun.

According to the National Center for Children in Poverty, for children in the highest-risk families and poorest communities, even the best early care and early learning opportunities will not be enough to help them perform on a level consistent with their more advantaged peers. However, a strong evidence base is showing that an intentional curriculum and effective teaching supports are promising pathways to increase the early literacy and math achievement of low-income preschool-age children.[94]

What does this mean in our work in preschool classrooms with regard to art – and even math and science? It means that we need to continue to strive and work towards providing children with the best art and creative opportunities to help them develop as 'whole', to be better equipped to deal with the curriculum in elementary school tomorrow.

"Creativity is as important as literacy."
-Sir Ken Robinson

CHAPTER 5

"We're building a dinosaur museum. The dinosaurs need to be tied up because the bones can get broken."

Logic In The Preschool Classroom

I HAVE BEEN FORTUNATE TO be able to spend time with young children as part of my job. I get to listen to the stories they create and laugh at the little jokes that I am privy to hearing. Needless to say, it's those stories that make my day! I remember a story about my young son, at age 4, who was really reluctant to clean up his Lego. "You always ask me to dismantle my Lego," he said. "When will you ask me to *mantle* it?" Children, between the ages of 2 and 7, do not have a clear sense of logic, and it is wonderful to be part of the process of their development as they move from pre-operational to concrete operational thought.

"Paper is a living thing since it comes from trees."

A short while ago, I had the opportunity to sit with the children at story time. The children were curious about living and non-living things, and through the story, 'The House for Hermit Crab', they explored this topic. They asked questions like "What makes a living thing living?" "Is a shell living or non-living?"

The children in this classroom are in a stage that Jean Piaget referred to as the preoperational stage. This stage has been described by him in his cognitive development theory as "a period between ages two and six, during which a child

117

learns to use language."[95] During this stage, the author states, children do not yet understand concrete logic, cannot mentally manipulate information and are unable to take the point of view of other people. In Piaget's view, due to the constraints of preoperational thought, preschoolers' first symbolic concepts are not as complete or as logical as are those of older children.[96]

The teacher passed out shells for the children to explore. As they explored the shells tactilely, the children wondered whether the shell was living or non-living. The children hypothesized about the characteristics of living things: they move; they breathe; they grow.

When asked for examples of living things, a child responded: "Paper is living because it comes from trees."

This kind of an over-generalization of a principle is typical of this stage of logical development in young children:

1. Trees are living.
2. Paper comes from trees.
3. Ergo, paper is living too.

As Susan Miller in her article on logical development in young children reflects, "Preschoolers at the preoperational stage of development use their perceptions of the environment, along with bits of information gathered during their past experiences, to understand their world. They base their understanding on what they see rather than on logic. They need to go through many illogical thinking processes before they can even begin to make logical sense of their world."[97]

On another occasion, a group of children found some geo-boards with rubber bands and proceeded to play with them. As they were playing, another child brought a basket of dinosaur skeletons to the table. Soon, the dinosaurs were "trapped" in rubber bands, ready to be "museum exhibits."

Overheard:

- *How do dinosaurs get in a museum?*
- *You find fossils.*
- *You find their bones and put them together.*
- *How do dinosaur babies come in bones?*
- *In eggs.*
- *Extinct means "dead".*
- *It means "never coming back".*
- *"We're building a dinosaur museum. The dinosaurs need to be tied up because the bones can get broken. "*
- *We're making a museum for all the dinosaurs to fight. They were alive and then they died and then they got in that. (pointing to the geo-board/rubber band construction)*
- *They were fighting. Then they died. Then they got in a hole. Then paleontologists dug them up and put them up the same way how they were fighting.*

Three key questions facilitate the process of inquiry in children:[98]

1. What do you think?
2. How could you find out or test your idea?
3. What did you learn or find out?

Children learn through a process of inquiry. As author Karen Worth states, "The cycle begins with an extended period of engagement where children explore the selected phenomenon and materials, experiencing what they are and can do, wondering about them, raising questions, and sharing ideas. This is followed by a more guided stage as questions are identified that might be investigated further." The purpose is to begin the process of more focused and deeper explorations involving prediction, planning, collecting, and recording data; organizing experiences; and looking for patterns and relationships that eventually can be shared and from which new questions may emerge.[99]

At this age, children's view of the world is normally very self-centered or egocentric and they see things from their own point of view. Their stories arise from their own experiences, or from their ideas of fantasy, and problem solving is usually a result of how they see things can be solved. They lack the ability to use abstract logic in their actions and in thinking and solving problems.

"Logic will get you from A to Z; imagination will get you everywhere."

-Albert Einstein

CHAPTER 6

"The world is a looking glass and gives back to every man the reflection of his own face."
-William Makepeace Thackeray

On the Importance of Mirrors in a Preschool Environment

CHILDREN LOVE TO LOOK AT themselves in a mirror. And no, not because they are narcissistic, but because they are just plain curious. And they are fascinated by what they see. Who is that creature I'm looking at? What do I see? Can I touch it? Wow... it moves! From watching children blowing on fogged up car windows, and leaving smudgy handprints as they draw on steamed up bathroom mirrors, we know that children are fascinated by reflections.

Babies begin their lives by liking what they see in the mirror. They show a preference for the human face. Cindy Brandon, an early childhood education professor at Toronto's Centennial College states, "They [mirrors] are inexpensive and fun...Babies are very attracted to faces." She adds "The baby moves, and the baby in the mirror moves too. It's like there is somebody there that they can pat and smile at, and they're smiling back." That interactive aspect is one of the reasons why Brandon feels that mirrors both encourage and provide an interesting window into babies' development.[100]

When placed in front of a mirror, even babies move their bodies and try and roll onto their side. They are curious about how they look, too! Toddlers walk up to mirrors and explore them tactically. This also helps in the development of more complex levels of understanding and reasoning. According to Harms, Clifford and Cryer, in their publication, '*Creating Early Learning Environments Into Practice*', children should be provided with an array of accessible materials. These accessible materials are age-appropriate materials, furnishings and equipment that children can reach and use independently. Harms *et al* state that children of all ages and abilities are attracted by aromas, sounds, colors, light, reflections and textures. When teachers add materials that invite touching, viewing and listening, children's experiences are broadened as they explore the environment. "Shiny mirrors, sparkling beads, transparent fabrics and reflected light focus children's attention on new ways of seeing the world."[101]

There are several superstitions in different cultures that surround this idea of showing a baby his/her reflection in the mirror. In some African cultures, mirrors are said to be a reflection of the soul. This happened because mirrors were often used in traditional witchcraft. In India, too, several people believe that young babies should never be allowed to see themselves in mirrors because they can "look into their souls."

Mirrors, however, contrary to superstitions, are great for babies and toddlers. Mirrors promote social and emotional development as babies interact with their own reflections. Mirrors are fun in a preschool classroom, too. They are versatile: they can be attached to the wall, placed on the floor, even attached to a ceiling. And they lend a dimension to an activity that enhances children's play and excites their curiosity. Using mirrors with a light table teaches them a little about the properties of light and deepens their exploration of not just light, but moving light. In an article written by Boyle regarding a study conducted by University of Berkeley's

Alison Gopnik, the author states, "...young kids think and learn about their surroundings much the way that scientists think and learn." She says, "They form hypotheses, test them, analyze their findings and learn from their actions and the actions of others – all in child's play.[102]

Another way that both parents and educators use mirrors is to help children handle their emotions. The Center on the Social and Emotional Foundations for Early Learning (CSEFEL) advises parents on the judicious use of mirrors to get children to express their emotions in ways that are healthy and developmentally appropriate.[103]

They tell educators and parents to play "Mirror, Mirror… what do I see?" with young children. The website states: 'Use a hand mirror or a mirror on the wall, play this game with your child. Look in the mirror and say "Mirror, mirror, what do I see?" Then make an emotion face. Follow by naming the emotion, by saying, "I see a sad Mommy/Teacher looking at me." Turn to your child and say "Your turn." Help your child remember the phrase "Mirror, mirror what do I see?" You may have to say it with your child. Then, tell your child to make a face and help him say the next sentence "I see a happy Patrick looking at me."

Teaching Feeling Words

We often only think of teaching common emotions like happy, sad, mad, etc. The author of the CSEFEL article highlights the fact that there are many other feeling words that children should learn to express, such as the following:[104]

- Brave
- Cheerful
- Bored
- Confused
- Surprised
- Curious
- Proud
- Disappointed
- Frustrated
- Embarrassed
- Silly
- Excited
- Uncomfortable
- Fantastic
- Worried
- Friendly
- Stubborn
- Generous
- Shy
- Ignored
- Satisfied
- Impatient
- Safe
- Important
- Relieved
- Interested
- Peaceful
- Jealous
- Overwhelmed
- Lonely
- Loving
- Confused
- Tense
- Angry
- Calm

Understanding emotions is a critical part of children's overall development, and mirrors are a great way to help them deal with their emotions and make better sense of them.

"Curiosity is the very basis of education and if you tell me that curiosity killed the cat, I say only the cat died nobly." -
-Arnold Edinborough

CHAPTER 7

"I am not a teacher, but an awakener."

-Robert Frost

On the Need for an Environment Rich With Provocations

TEACHERS DON'T JUST TEACH. THEY awaken. That's the job we teachers have – to awaken the curiosity in children, to pique their interest. And the best way to do that in a preschool classroom is by having 'provocations' in the environment. Provocations are very common in a Reggio-inspired classroom. They are thoughtfully set up materials intended to extend and expand the learning of children.

I pay a lot of attention to the aesthetics in an environment. Aesthetics, in the context that I have used it in, can be defined as the appreciation of a pleasant and special sensory experience (usually visual, aural, or tactile). However, as well as being pleasing to the senses, aesthetic objects or situations often involve other features that are pleasing to the cognitive faculties: repetition, pattern, continuity, clarity, dexterity, elaboration or variation of a theme, contrast, balance, and proportion.[105]

When environments are set up in an inviting and aesthetically pleasing manner, children derive a special sensory experience from their play. In all of the areas in the classroom, I use provocations.

Provocations spark new questions and more ideas, and invite children to touch, to explore and to be curious. They make the mundane interesting and add new dimensions to the classroom. The Reggio approach sees provocations as "...important aspects of stretching the children's learning. Teachers provoke the children to investigate further about a given topic by providing different materials and ideas for them to use."[106]

Setting up a preschool classroom has in some ways become so run-of-the-mill and pedestrian: you wipe down a table, tip a basket of blocks on it, and voila...you have a 'setup'.

But 'setting up' is so much more. It requires keen observation and patience; passion and a love of beauty; interest in children's learning and a great sense of imagination. 'Setting up' can take up to an hour of lovingly arranging things in a classroom. All just so you can hear the "Aaah" as soon as children walk in. You see the wonder in their eyes, enjoy their tactile exploration of the material, and finally, celebrate when they rejoice in their creations and new knowledge. That's what setups should be – and that's what 'awakening' children's learning should look like.

According to authors Katherina Danko McGhee and Sharon Shaffer, "When children express preferences for colors, shapes, sounds, tastes and textures, they are making aesthetic choices."[107] They say that aesthetic experiences can enhance cultural sensitivity, promote language development, and improve the quality of young children's own art making. The Reggio Emilia philosophy believes that creativity (in children) emerges from multiple experiences. Providing children with the basic resources is great; however, equipping the environment with materials that extend the learning helps children develop their creativity.

What does all of this require? As I had mentioned earlier, it takes some time and some planning. You could very easily put out eight colors of paint in little cups for children to paint with; however, by adding the work of an artist as a provocation and by choosing only those colors of paint that the artist has used, you then 'awaken' the learning in the child and move him or her to a different level of learning and appreciation.

I set out a book on jeweled bugs with metallic paint, tempera paint and shiny fabric. The results were amazing; the questions were awesome, and the learning was just wonderful.

The children asked:

- *Did the jewel bug get some glitter?*
- *How did its wings get so shiny?*
- *Is the shiny wing different from the wings inside?*
- *Does a jewel bug make its own colors?*
- *How does someone make glitter paint?*

By allowing children to experiment with different colors and different textures, we gave them a better understanding about understanding the work of artist: they learned to work with light and dark colors; they learned to use different media: i.e. fabric, paint and glue in the same piece of art; and they learned to work with paints of different densities.

This kind of set up can be used in every area of the classroom: the block area, the light table, the book area etc. It's exciting for children to see material displayed in this manner. It invites their participation. It enhances their learning. I have had 3-year-old children point to an artist's work and ask me, "Is that a Jackson Pollock?" In every manner possible, it IS the way to set up an environment conducive to learning.

So for teachers: No more dumping plastic fish in a water table because you think that children are learning a lot through that. It's moving from dumping to thoughtfully setting up. No more just leaving a book on the table to be read. It's putting out puppets and props to extend the language of a child. This kind of thoughtful set up of provocations in the environment will move children to a different place – a place that is ripe with materials intended for their exploration, a place that is ripe for discovery.

"When you teach a child something you take away forever his chance of discovering it for himself.

-Jean Piaget

CHAPTER 8

"Never laugh at live dragons."
– J.R.R. Tolkien

The Power of Storytelling and its Place in a Preschool Classroom

Act 1, Scene 1: Large dinosaur stomps through the shrubs and roars loudly.
Somewhere else, in another preschool classroom:
Act 1, Scene 1: Baby cries, "Waaah." A bowl of food is prepared in great haste.
And in another preschool, in a far off country:
Act1, Scene 1: Crocodile swims stealthily in the water and suddenly snaps its lethal jaws. Snap, snap, snap!

Children *need* stories – stories that are fun, stories that are rich with imagination, stories that stir their senses! When children are very young, they make sense of the world around them by enacting stories that remind them of their homes and lives, or those that help them deal with their unspoken fears.

Psychologist Sandra Russ identified a number of different cognitive and affective processes that are associated with pretend play.[108] Her research dealing with play involves fantasy, make-believe, symbolism, organization, cognitive integration of seemingly separate content, and divergent thinking (the ability to come up with many different ideas and story themes). Is it then surprising that young children gravitate towards this area of a classroom first?

One day, I watched as the children played outdoors. They had just woken up from their nap, and were happily engaged in playing at the play dough table.

Suddenly, a drop of water landed on a child's face, and she looked up startled. She looked up at the clouds, and pointed to them. "It's raining!" she said, and she ran to get an umbrella.

She soon had a whole lot of children running around the play yard following her as she looked for an umbrella. They ran around the yard, each one following the other and they chanted, "It's raining, it's raining!"

They looked for places to hide in, to protect themselves from the drizzle. As they ran from hiding place to hiding place, their glee was perceptible. One of them found a bunch of fishing nets in the sensory table, and suddenly, they all had 'umbrellas'. They held their umbrellas above their heads and ran around, saying, "It's raining, it's raining."

The children were able to represent objects and events (umbrella and the rain) symbolically. In an article on '*Spontaneous Play*', the author, Fergus Hughes states that cognitive theorists have long supported the view that spontaneous imaginative play facilitates children's intellectual development.[109]

The author stresses that Piaget maintained pretend play of this kind often arises from symbolic play, and these games "are initially imbued with play symbolism, but tend later to constitute genuine adaptations (mechanical constructions, etc.), or solutions to problems and intelligent creations." [110] He argued that spontaneous play facilitates intellectual development in that it can lead to discoveries about the physical environment.

I enjoy watching children engaged in fantasy play – cooking, dressing up and washing babies. While this kind of play is lovely to watch, it's important to understand that is in fact essential for the healthy growth and development of a child. Vivian Paley, well-known author and advocate for children's play states, "Play is, in fact, a complex occupation, requiring practice in dialogue, exposition, detailed imagery, social engineering, literary allusion, and abstract thinking. Being both work and love for young children, play is absolutely essential for their health and welfare."[111]

On one occasion, in the United States, I was invited to sit down at a table with the children and was offered some 'fish' to eat. I declined, letting the children know that I am a vegetarian. We then had a detailed discussion of what that really meant: "You don't even eat fish?" Another child offered me a cheeseburger." Don't worry, I'll take the meat off." A third offered me my vegetables with some hot sauce. (How did he know that was my favorite?)

These young children were practicing very advanced skills of empathy, showing me a lot of caring as they took care of my food preferences. It's no wonder that empathy is learned in the preschool classroom, in situations such as these. In an article on fantasy play, the author states, "When your child engages in pretend (or dramatic) play, he is actively experimenting with the social and emotional roles of life. It is through cooperative play, he learns how to take turns, share responsibility, and creatively problem-solve. When your child pretends to be different characters, he has the experience of 'walking in someone else's shoes,' which helps teach the important moral development skill of empathy. It is normal for young children to see the world from their own egocentric point of view, but through maturation and cooperative play, a child will begin to understand the feelings of others."[112]

I observed the children at play, and recorded their stories to try and interpret the learning that had occurred. "Listening to children play," Vivian Paley states, "we become reporters and anecdotists, passing along our accounts and searching for meaning in what we see and hear... Play gives us the opportunity to seek its own meaning in a way that no other subject can, because in play the subjects are always seeking to know what they are inventing."[113]

It's interesting to listen to the conversations that children have when they are cooking or eating pretend foods. It's amazing that in this kind of play, children take risks in eating foods they never would eat in real life: broccoli, spicy foods, green vegetables... and even strange combinations of foods (strawberry-lemon-chocolate-sand cupcakes)!

Research has found that parents' food preferences are linked to their children's food preferences. The author of the article states that we are more likely to prepare the foods that we enjoy, so our children are more familiar with that group of foods than others. Familiarity with foods, the author stresses, is key, as a child may need to be exposed to new foods more than 10 times before they try it.[114]

It is through this fantasy play that children engage in that they practice their language and literacy and grow their vocabulary. Fantasy play is an indispensable ingredient of authentic childhood!

Sometimes, in situations where budgets are tight, or in areas of extreme poverty where there isn't much in terms of objects for fantasy play, even a mere show and tell activity can pave the way to both play and learning. Some classrooms and preschools have an hour of show and tell in the morning as a way to encourage young children to integrate literacy and oral language. Learning about and practicing speaking about an object helps a child move from receptive literacy and language to productive literacy, an important cognitive shift.

Having miniatures to pretend play with, adds a dimension of fantastic thinking to the ordinary and mundane activity of show and tell.

What I have noticed about regions that are afflicted with great poverty is that you cannot really ask a child to 'bring' an object from home to show and tell. Objects are few and far between, and so often, the child's imaginative oral capacity (fantastic thinking) remains stunted.

A nice addition to a classroom where resources are low is to have a 'magic box' – a shoe box with small, random objects that would encourage language production in a child. I have often bought small toys – combs, Barbie and other doll accessories etc., from flea markets and thrift stores, and filled shoe boxes with them. Each morning, I have brought out my magic box from which a child can pick out an object and speak about it. What this does is that it increases creative language use, the use of subjunctives, past and future tenses, and adjectives.

Another important facet of socio-dramatic play is story dictation. This is when a child tells a story (dictating it to an adult) or describes an event to a teacher who transcribes the story for him/her. Through this process of story dictation, an extension of the show and tell activity, although the child is not actually doing the writing, the child develops her language, and in this case, pre-literacy skills in the process. According to author Vivian Paley, story dictation serves as the "conduit through which the uniqueness of each child's contribution can be recognized and valued."[115]

Sometimes, teachers use the upper case to transcribe the stories that children tell, and at other times, the lower case. In fact, teachers are always confused about whether to use the upper case or the lower case when introducing the alphabet to young children. Personally, I have always picked the upper case first only because the upper case is largely made up of straighter lines, while the lower case is comprised of lots of circles. When children's hand muscles are developing, curves and circles are a lot more difficult for them to create. Besides, the child will most probably be exposed to print on storefronts and hoardings, most of which are written in the upper case script.

In preschool environments, we see children play. They play with blocks, they play with cars, they play with plastic animals, and they play with dolls. While it might seem surprising that children always gravitate towards fantasy play, it's important to understand how important fantasy play is in their cognitive growth. Both Vygotsky and Piaget viewed pretend play as the area "where a child performs at the best level of his abilities." Play is a safe place to try things. During pretend or symbolic play, children 'try on' a variety of roles and through their play; they develop socially and emotionally as well as cognitively. Vygotsky believed that during social pretend play (that is, symbolic play that children carry out with someone else), the play context provides 'scaffolding' for the child's development through his zone.[116]

When the child pretends to be in another role, for example, when a girl pretends to be a mother taking care of a sick baby, she is trying out responsibilities that she has seen her mother carry out, thus stretching herself beyond what she really can do.

Vygotsky also believed that in pretend play, a child is required "to stay within the rules" of the play game and act according to the "roles and plot." He states, for example, "A child may be frightened, but if she is pretending to be a superhero, she must act at not being frightened." Thus, according to Vygotsky, "Social pretend play helps children develop in the social, emotional and in the cognitive domains of development."[117]

In the area of language and literacy, many educators use flannel boards to help scaffold children's learning. Debbie

Sternklar, in her article on the use of flannel boards in preschool environments states "Flannel boards aid in the teaching of visual literacy – learning to look and construct meaning from objects." This is important because "Children use personal connections to enable the decoding of visual representations of their experiences. They will recognize a picture of a cat, drawn by different illustrators as a "symbol" for a cat, and know that it is not a cat, but represents one. Later they learn that letters represent ideas when assembled into words."[118]

A flannel board provides children with the ability to comprehend and appreciate a story visually, auditorily, and kinesthetically. In many preschool environments in India, in South Africa, and in the US, I have painted story boards on the walls of the classrooms – something like the flannel boards we use for storytelling. One of the focuses that educators have for children is the increase in the use of de-contextualized language[119] when children talk about objects/events beyond "here and now." It is through encouraging pretend play that children learn and develop new language. Here are some strategies used by educators to increase the use of de-contextualized language:

- Develop and use scripted dialogue to model appropriate language forms and social interaction for selected scenarios.
- Model stories that provide rich detail for children so they can learn more about typical experiences in this dramatic scenario.
- Provide opportunities for re-telling of stories/ or for using the new vocabulary in varied ways.
- Introduce vocabulary words and concepts related to play theme.
- Make ties between immediate experience and past events.

Imagination was not always valued as much as it is now. Shirley Wang, in her article 'The Power of Magical Thinking', states that "...imagination was thought of as a way for children to escape from reality, and once they reached a certain age, it was believed they would push fantasy aside and deal with the real world."[120] But, increasingly, child-development experts are recognizing the importance of imagination and the role it plays in understanding reality.

So I create sea murals complete with octopus, sea horses, sea stars, and small schools of fish. This encourages them to be able to visualize these creatures, and use their imagination in their play. There was an instance once, in a school in San Jose, where I painted a mural of sea creatures. I watched as a little girl went right up to the wall and began to make "swimming motions." She saw me watching her, and she said, "Teacher Jayanti, I'm a mermaid. I'm swimming with the fish."

When I see children engaged in fantasy play, I am reminded of the song by America: 'You can do magic; you can have everything that you desire...' And it's true. This magical thinking truly does help children have or become anything or anybody that they desire! Give children the tools, and they *will* do magic!

When we provide young children with literacy-related materials, props for socio-dramatic play and multiple opportunities for them to use language, children make rapid strides in their literacy development.

"We are making poison. And because you are vegetarian, we are making vegetarian poison."

WHAT'S COOKING? APPARENTLY, QUITE A lot in the preschool sandbox!

As I went from one preschool classroom to another, I saw children in the sandbox, deeply immersed in cooking. Not cooking the way an adult would imagine, but rather cooking in a largely metaphoric way. They used the materials available to them that range from sand, rocks and leaves, to water and soap, and conjure up yummy dishes...and sometimes, they cooked with nothing at all. It's just imaginary. That's the power of children's metaphoric thinking.

Metaphorical thinking – our instinct not just for describing, but for comprehending one thing in terms of another, for equating one with another – shapes our view of the world, and is essential to how we communicate, learn, discover, and invent. Metaphor is a way of thought long before it is a way with words.

The author of the article states that "children, it turns out, are on the one hand skilled and intuitive weavers of original metaphors and, on the other, utterly (and, often, humorously) stumped by common adult metaphors, revealing that metaphor is both evolutionarily rooted and culturally constructed." She adds that "as children's cognition develops and their understanding of the world evolves, their metaphorical range becomes more expansive — something equally true of us grown-ups."[121]

Their creations oscillated between cooking 'real' food and also pretend food. I watched as the children cooked in the sandbox, using cups and bowls, stirring the mixture of sand and water rather fervently. Then, after cooking some real food in their classroom, the children's ideas and needs also changed. Now, they needed an oven; they needed more real tools, to continue to make pretend food.

"We are sharks. Watch: I'm vomiting."
Teacher: *Why are you vomiting?*

"Because I ate 'Person Food'. I ate an electric camera."

"Fantasy is a necessary ingredient in living, it's a way of looking at life through the wrong end of a telescope."
-Dr. Seuss

CHAPTER 9

"It's my birthday when the birthday hat comes on my head!"

Calendar Time and the Morning Routine

Overheard:
"Tomorrow never comes. When it's today, it's yesterday, so tomorrow never comes." "Because tomorrow is Saturday and Saturday never comes."

"Sunday, Monday, Tuesday, Wednesday, Thursday, Friday, Saturday..."

MORNING MEETING TIME IS THE same in most of the preschools that I have visited: they start the day with calendar time. The children recite the days of the week first in English, and then in their home language (Swat or Shangan, Spanish, Hindi, Kannada, Marathi); then they recite the months of the year, again in the languages of the classroom; then they identify colors and shapes on the wall.

And then they sing a couple of songs, frequently the National Anthem or religious songs. This whole routine can take up to half an hour. In some of the preschools, the children remain standing for the entire time, and some of the children still have their backpacks on their backs. In other schools, the children remain sitting, all huddled together. Some seem to recite the days of the week, or the months of the year like parrots; others seem disinterested.

This brings me to the question, why is it so important to do calendar time in preschool? We already know that preschool children do not have a well-developed understanding of time. I have been told by a dear friend's son that his birthday "will be when his birthday hat comes on his head", and by another little girl that her birthday is yesterday, on Tuesday.

Beneke, Ostrosky & Katz, in their article on temporal understanding in preschool children, point out that adults use calendars to mark and measure time, such as scheduling appointments, remembering birthdays, and anticipating upcoming special events (spring break, a basketball tournament). They do however stress the fact that there is little evidence that calendar activities that mark extended periods of time (a month, a week) are meaningful for children below first grade.[122]

In their opinion, to participate meaningfully in calendar activities, young children must understand that time is sequential. The sequences include yesterday, today, and tomorrow; morning, afternoon, and evening; Sunday, Monday, Tuesday, and so on. Thus, young children can talk about things that have happened or will happen, but they cannot yet understand or talk about these events in terms of units of time (days, weeks) or sequence. This child development knowledge draws into question the usefulness of calendar activities for children under the age of 6.

There are definite benefits to rote memorization and routine; however, this can also be achieved through songs and rhymes that have little to do with the recitation of the days of the week or the months of the year. The teachers also cover topics like colors and shapes. Some of them just point to papers pasted on the walls that have colored shapes drawn on them. When we think of Gardner's Multiple Intelligences, this kind of teaching only appeals to the ones who are linguistically or logical-mathematical. What about the rest of the children whose dominant intelligence may not be mathematical, I wonder.

A Kaleidoscope of Children

There is so much pinned up on the walls of many of these classrooms that it seems to distract the children from the function that it should really serve. Children try in vain to pick out shapes and colors from the huge array of papers and charts displayed on the walls.

In a recent study published by Carnegie Mellon, it was found that although maps, number lines, shapes, artwork and other materials tend to cover elementary classroom walls, this might end up disrupting attention and learning in young children. It was found that children in overly decorated classrooms were more distracted, spent more time off-task and demonstrated smaller learning gains than when the decorations were removed.[123]

The general idea is to take a fresh look at the cognitive learning that happens during a morning circle or routine, and what we have noticed is that there is a high emphasis on rote learning and repetition. Pasi Sahlberg, a Finnish education official and author of '*Finnish Lessons: What Can the World Learn from Educational Change in Finland*', says "Teaching and learning have traditionally been conceptualized as linear, deterministic procedures." In his opinion, "Innovation is an organic entity. Teaching and learning in schools should rely on principles of active participation, social interaction and reflection."[124]

"It's Not How Smart You Are – It's How You're Smart!"
-Howard Gardner

CHAPTER 10

Bears Can't Be Girls

Examining the Influences on Gender Development in Young Children

WE ALREADY KNOW THAT YOUNG children have their own understanding of gender – of what it means to be a boy or a girl – and this is hugely influenced by their families, by culture and society, and today, more than ever, by media. A few years ago, during circle time, I was going to play the Bear Hunt song[125] on the CD player, and I announced to the children that I would be the bear that would chase all of the children. Before I could press 'play', one of the children stopped me in my tracks with: "You can't be a bear; bears are boys."

This was the conversation that ensued:

Child 1: *No. Girls can't be bears. Bears are only boys.*
Teacher: *So when you are being chased by a bear, are you going to stop and ask, "Are you a girl bear or a boy bear?"*
Child 2: *Bears are boy bears and girl bears.*
Child 3: *You know that all cows are girls and all bulls are boys.*
Child 4: *When you see a girl bear, it has eyes that look like a girl (she gestures to show long curling eyelashes).*
Child 5: *Bears can be small, medium and large.*
Child 6: *Boy bears have dark hands and girl bears have*

light hands. And their claws are medium in the mama bear and big claws in the boy bear.

Child 7: *You also know from the knees because their legs are really long. Yeah. A boy bear has short and wide legs.*

Child 5: *In their mouths, they have really sharp teeth. When they eat, the boy bear's claws go right through the body and the girl bear's just go halfway through. And when the boy bear goes into the meat, it tears the meat when it's eating. A bear is a boy and a girl bear is a different kind of bear.*

Child 1: *When boy bears stomp, it makes the trees fall and the earth shake. When people want to catch the bear, they look at the footprints and they can tell if it's a girl bear or a boy bear.*

Child 2: *you don't want to go next to a bear when there are baby bears next to it. The bear with babies is a girl bear.*

Child 5: *If there's a bear with cubs, then it's a mama bear.*

Child 8: *Boy bears are black and girl bears are brown.*

Child 5: *the footprints of boy and girl bears are different. The boy bear's (footprints) are big and the girl bear's (footprints) are medium.*

Where did these messages about gender come in to a child's mind? How did the children know whether girl bears have curling lashes or that boy bears stomp and the earth shakes? It is really important for us as educators to understand the impact that gender stereotypes have on young children. These ideas and concepts of what a girl can do (or not do) and what a boy can or cannot do are ingrained in children, as research says, sometimes, even before birth. Olaiya E Aina and Petronella A. Cameron in their article on gender formation in preschool children state that stereotypes are fairly well developed by 5 years of age, and become rigidly defined between 5 and 7 years of age. This, in their opinion, makes "… the preschool years a critical period to deal with gender stereotypes."[126] The authors go on to say that these kinds of stereotypes limit potential growth and development.

The early gender bias experiences that children encounter can shape their:[127]

- attitudes and beliefs related to their development of interpersonal and intrapersonal relationships,
- access to education equality,
- participation in the corporate work world, as well as
- stifling their physical and psychological well being.

As educators, we need to have meaningful conversations with children to understand where they are in their comprehension and internalization of such biases. By gently challenging these biases, and giving them different perspectives and ways to look at ideas, we help children grow and develop to be more capable adults – and definitely more capable of resisting bullying in the later years.

After we had the bear conversation, we sat down to discuss the gender issue connected with bears. We talked about male and female roles in society, and reaffirmed to children that boys, *and* girls can both do what they wished to do: they could both become firefighters, doctors or policemen; they could both grow up to be nurturing parents of children of their own; or they could both become 'big' and indeed, fly to the moon!

Cars, trucks, planes and helicopters… Are these really 'boy' things?

RECENTLY, I HAVE NOTICED THAT many of the boys seem to gravitate towards cars, trucks, helicopters, and things that have wheels. This set me thinking about toys and gender. Do boys really prefer to play with trucks and cars? Is it something that is only influenced by media, or is there any evidence to suggest that there might be some evolutionary reason for this play?

There are many suggestions on why part of this might be evolutionary. Certainly, in some cultures, people might have expectations that boys should behave like 'boys', and girls, like 'girls'. Are boys more physical because we encourage them? Probably. However, as author Gwen Dewar ('*Girl Toys, Boy Toys, and Parenting*') states, that doesn't mean behavior is entirely determined by social factors. She adds that child's play is also influenced by prenatal development.[128]

In a study conducted by Janet Hasset et al at the Yerkes National Primate Research Center, Emory University, Atlanta, it was found that gender differences in rhesus monkey toy preferences (male and female) parallel or mimic those of young children.

The experiment, conducted on male and female rhesus monkeys showed that although the young monkeys were not socialized into playing with gender specific toys, male monkeys showed a greater preference for wheeled toys.

What are the best toys for children? Girl toys, boy toys or gender-neutral toys? Cars? Dolls? Nintendo Wii?

OVER THE PAST FEW DECADES, our society has had so many different toys and gadgets for young children, from hand held DS devices to the Nintendo Wii. The truth, however, is that children are really content with the simple toys that our parents gave us: pots and pans in the kitchen, and plastic buckets in the bathtub.

I love the article by Angie Dorrell on the best toys for children. She says, "Some toys and materials are a better choice for young children than others... The best toys actively engage children in many areas of development and can be used in a variety of ways, depending on the child's interests, ability, and imagination."[129]

She adds that toys that encourage children's imagination help them know that the world is a diverse and wonderful place. She cautions parents not to let the hype sway their decision especially when "children may clamor for the 'toy of the moment.'"

I have observed children playing in the sand box and at the water table. Sand and water toys are what we call 'open-ended' toys. Toys such as buckets and pails, funnels, beakers and spades allow children to freely explore the properties of sand and water. Through their exploration of the materials, they learn concepts such as size, weight, measurement, and other science and math concepts. Of course, they also get to exercise their imagination! I once overheard one group of children as they were busy burying a plastic dinosaur in sand: "We are putting sand on the dinosaurs so they go to dinosaur jail and become extinct and you can't see them anymore."

Jonathan Liu,[130] in his article on the 5 best toys of all times touches on some of my favorites. These are, in fact gender neutral. They fall into neither the girl toy nor boy toy bucket and are widely enjoyed by both.

1. Stick - In Liu's words, "This versatile toy is a real classic — chances are your great-great-grandparents played with one, and your kids have probably discovered it for themselves as well. It's a required ingredient for Stickball, of course, but it's so much more. Stick works really well as a poker, digger and reach-extender." He cautions parents (and teachers) that often times, the stick becomes a weapon.

2. Box - Another toy on his list (also my favorite) is quite versatile. The Box comes in a variety of shapes and sizes. Boxes, he mentions, "can be turned into furniture or a kitchen playset." He adds that you can turn your kids into cardboard robots. "A large box can be used as a fort or house and a smaller box can be used to hide away a special treasure."

The third one is my least favorite.

3. String - He does caution adults that String is not intended for toddlers and babies: it is a strangulation hazard. However, when used properly your kids can really have a ball with String.

4. Cardboard Tube - Cardboard Tubes are also very versatile, but like the Stick, they often end up as swords or guns.

5. Dirt (I will add sand, or mud, as it is referred to in different parts of the world, to this one) This one is a favorite with all of the children I have worked with. Dirt, as the author puts it, "has been around longer than any of the other toys on this list, and shows no signs of going away." Some studies have shown that kids who play with Dirt have stronger immune systems than those who don't.

"I'd like to see where boys and girls end up if they get equal encouragement - I think we might have some differences in how leadership is done."

-Sheryl Sandberg

CHAPTER 11

"Yuck! This is ooey, gooey and glue-y!"

Sensory Development in Young Children

GLUE HOLDS A VERY IMPORTANT place in my classroom – glue in squeeze bottles, glue mixed with paint, glue in small containers. Children have daily experiences with glue, paint and play dough in my classrooms. It is through this language of messy media that children express themselves in a variety of ways. Kate Martin, in '*Encounters: A Reggio Emilia Dialogue Within New Zealand*' states, "Children go back and forth between verbal dialogue and graphic representations, but may also move to different symbolic languages, such as paint, wire or clay, requiring new interpretations of their ideas." "This process," the author adds, "recognizes and provides opportunity for strengths of young children to be utilized, and demonstrates the many potentials and capabilities that children bring to their learning."[131]

There's something magical about clay. Author Robert Schirrmacher describes the experience best when he says, "A line with a crayon is unchangeable, however, a long coil of clay can become a snake, then a bowl, then a snowman. The possibilities are endless and children enjoy this freedom to transform their creations."[132] And it's these endless possibilities that children are immersed in creating.

It's fascinating to watch children as they work with clay. Younger children seem to work with the clay with tentative movements— first poking and touching it with just one finger. Then, as they grow comfortable with the medium, they use their hands to 'cup' the clay.

With the preschoolers, working with clay can become a whole body experience. I have often watched as they pound and pinch the clay, using their whole hands, or their pincer grasp. For some it can be a sensory experience— they add water to the clay and revel in the sensory nature of the clay. In one child's words, "the clay becomes "slimy, wet and squishy."

Stages of clay making:[133] (these are not set in stone…)

Stage 1: At about age 2, children enjoy playing and experimenting with clay. They do not try to create specific objects, but rather are trying to understand what clay is and what they can do with it. The experience is all about the process, and never about the product.

Stage 2: Around 3 years old, children become more deliberate in their clay experimentations. "As scientists, they put clay to a series of tests by rolling, pinching, tearing, pulling, and poking it. By physically acting on clay, they discover its properties."

Stage 3: At around 4 years of age, children begin to take their scientific studies to the next step by bringing their clay forms to life. Rolled balls can become snowmen with feelings and thoughts of their own.

Stage 4: At about 5 years old, children have the confidence and ability to come to the clay table with an idea of what it is they want to make. At this stage children learn to problem solve and to come up with creative solutions to their own ideas.

It's always a treat to watch young children manipulate play dough. They roll, squish, press, squeeze and pummel the dough. They make long snakes, squash flat patties, and cut little pieces, molding the dough in their hands. The dough often takes on a life of its own!

Mallary I Swartz, in her article on play dough,[134] states that play dough allows children of all ages to express themselves through art and to engage in dramatic play as they interact with the materials and with others.

She emphasizes that young children learn best through manipulation of materials in which they can see the effects they have on the world around them. Many of these experiences, as we already know, come through play. Creative experiences with materials like play dough offer children many valuable learning opportunities, and address all domains of development- physical, social emotional and cognitive.

Children enjoy manipulating play dough and as they work the dough in their hands, they build their muscles in their hands. This muscle development helps them write with better muscle control in the later years.

By adding material (such as scissors) to the play dough table, teachers help children gain better control of scissors. Children need a lot of practice with scissors, and cutting play dough with scissors help them hone this skill. According to Anne Zachary, author of an article on scissor use,[135] cutting with scissors requires the skill of hand separation, which is the ability to use the thumb, index, and middle fingers separately from the pinkie and ring fingers.

This takes both time and practice, and there's no better place than the preschool environment to perfect this skill! We know that right from birth, children learn about the world through their senses: through touch, taste, smell, sight, and hearing. Sensory play also contributes in crucial ways to brain development.[136]

So, providing a variety of sensory experiences (paint, water, sand, fabric, different textures, colors) that pique their curiosity is very essential, because infants thrive on sensory stimuli. It is common for educators to give them experiences with finger paint and with glue. Since young infants and toddlers tend to eat glue and paint, it's prudent to use home-made glue and paint. While many might claim that store bought paints are non- toxic, it's important to know that non-toxic doesn't necessarily mean safe.

We often see this: after a while of exploring the paint with their hands, the children begin to get paint on their arms and faces too. This kind of messy play, according to Patricia Hughes, stimulates the senses. In her article on messy play, she adds that the tactile experience gained during messy play helps children experience a variety of textures. During messy play, babies and toddlers are developing eye hand coordination and fine motor skills. What looks like a mess on the surface is truly a learning experience for your child.[137]

On one of my visits to a classroom in the United States, I watched the children deeply engrossed in making sticky mud. (And I am fortunate to be able to share the recipe: 1 part sand – very dry sand; two parts water – very hot water; then, just mix it up!) The sticky mud was very necessary to 'kill' the sharks that were swimming in the water.

When children play, they integrate their senses, and they integrate their domains of learning to make sense of the world that they live in. Alison Gopnik of UC Berkeley describes this phenomenon as children's scientific thinking.[138] She states that when engaged in what looks like child's play, preschoolers are actually behaving like scientists. According to a new report in the journal, Science, they are forming hypotheses, running experiments, calculating probabilities and deciphering causal relationships about the world.

The children discussed why sharks needed to be killed. "Sharks are not bad – not all bad. Baby sharks are good. Baby dolphins are good. Baby whales are good. They don't know too much. But when baby sharks grow big, they learn too much. They learn that they can eat people. They learn to be bad. So we have to kill sharks." The children then combined the pleasures of playing in the sand and water with socio-dramatic play to engage in a story (with real props—a set of shark teeth!)

The children examined the shark teeth with a great deal of curiosity.

Here's what they said:

"Be careful, that's sharp."

"That's from a great white shark or a leopard shark..."

"Or a big shark..."

"It has so many teeth..."

"That's a shark skeleton..."

Our preschoolers have a natural curiosity and wonder about the world around them. They examine, look, touch, taste, hypothesize and then draw conclusions. All this is a natural part of the scientific process!

"I would like to paint the way a bird sings."

-Claude Monet

CHAPTER 12

"The old order changeth"

From STEM to DREAMER

"THE OLD ORDER CHANGETH, YIELDING place to new…" said Lord Tennyson. This is very true especially in the field of education. We have had philosophers like Dewey, and Montessori, Piaget and Erickson tell us about how children develop. And as the years have gone by, we have added to those ideas, and also subtracted from them. Over the last few years, it's been the 'in' thing to align oneself with acronyms, and many schools jumped on that bandwagon to become STEM schools (Science, Technology, Engineering and Math.)

This trend also extended itself to the preschool arena, and before we knew it, it was like the Baby Einstein phenomenon – everyone wanted a STEM preschool so we could produce engineers, scientists and doctors. I have always maintained that if I have to be associated with an acronym, it should be that I am a "DREAMER."

- D - Diversity in Early Childhood Education (ECE)
- R - Respect for children, families, and ECE professionals
- E - Emergent curriculum
- A - the Arts
- M - Music & Movement
- E - Engineering, Math & Science
- R - a Robust and fun curriculum

I read two articles, both of which validated my beliefs, and my thoughts. As everyone knows, Finland's education system is considered an exemplary model for the rest of the world, and they are on the verge of making some major changes.

According to Rebecca Klein, author of 'Finland's Schools Are Overhauling the Way They Do Things. Here's How'[139], the schools are moving to a 'Phenomenon Based Teaching Model' where the National Curriculum Framework serves as a broad outline for educators, and requires that for at least a couple of weeks each year, educators use phenomenon-based teaching – an approach that emphasizes broad interdisciplinary topics rather than single-subject classes. (And doesn't that sound so much like the Reggio or the Project Approach, both amazing models to adopt in the ECE environment?)

The next change that Finland is adopting is this: Finland's students will be involved in planning these new, interdisciplinary projects, and will be expected to evaluate their success. (This sounds so much like Betty Jones' Emergent Curriculum, where curriculum is negotiated and planned by children, based on their interests.)

And last but not the least, Finnish classrooms will literally be redesigned under the new curriculum framework. Instead of a traditional classroom, where kids sit in rows of desks in front of a teacher, students in the near future will work in clusters to promote communication skills. Over the past few months I have been harping on the need for preschool teachers to move away from giving children individual projects and sheets of A4 sized paper to color on. Teachers give large sheets of butcher paper, canvas, and even old bedsheets for children to use for art experiences. We need to move from the very self- centered world of "I-me-my" to the more inclusive, collaborative world of "we-us-ours."

The other headline that caught my eye was this in the Washington Post: 'We don't need more STEM majors. We need more STEM majors with liberal arts training.'[140]

As the author, Loretta Jackson-Hayes says, "Our culture has drawn an artificial line between art and science, one that did not exist for innovators like Leonardo da Vinci and Steve Jobs. Leonardo's curiosity and passion for painting, writing, engineering and biology helped him triumph in both art and science." This artificial line didn't exist in the preschool environment either. Today's world needs to go back to the old order of Dewey: "Education is not preparation for life; Education is life itself."

We don't need to educate our young children to be engineers, scientists and astronauts: we need to prepare them to be citizens of tomorrow's world, and that requires us to look way beyond STEM studies in early childhood.

"Education is the most powerful weapon which you can use to change the world."

-Nelson Mandela

Block building is essential for children to learn and practice their spatial thinking.

Early Pictorialism in a picture drawn by a three year old- "I drew a giant scorpion."

Education begins the gentleman but reading, good
company and reflection must finish him.

It is all
about the
process.

Manipulatives are tools that help enhance and strengthen fine motor skills. They exist in most classrooms in the form of blocks Legos and small cars.

Open ended process based art.

Pretend Play in the Preschool Years

Math in preschool; Recognizing and forming geometrical shapes and designs.

Sorting and categorizing and estimating are essential skills for later success in science.

There is something magical about clay.

Block Play promotes creative, divergent problem solving

Categorizing and practicing early math in the sandbox

Classroom provocations provoke interest.

Learning math through creating and exploring patterns.

CHAPTER 13

"Your assumptions are your windows on the world. Scrub them off every once in a while, or the light won't come in."
-Isaac Asimov

On the Asking of Open-Ended Questions

THE BEST PART OF THE job of an educator, or in fact the job of a parent is listening to the wonderful stuff that children say. I go to work each day, wondering what gem I will be treated to on that day…and the rewards are plenty. The way to elicit information when children say things to us is to ask them 'tell me more' questions, or open-ended questions. One day, I was sitting and playing with a little 2-year-old, and she looked at my earrings and said, "Look, you are wearing dancing earrings!" I felt my earring and realized that I was wearing earrings that resembled musical chords. I asked the little girl to tell me more about why she thought that they were dancing earrings, and she said, "Because they have music!"

When we ask children these 'tell-me-more' questions, the answers open up a world of possibilities; besides, there are no wrong answers.

Here are some open-ended questions to ask of children:[141]

- Tell me about your picture.
- What else can you do with the play dough?
- Why do you think this happened?

A Kaleidoscope of Children

- What do you think would happen if . . . ?
- Is there another way to . . . ?

Lisa Wilkin, in her article on open-ended questions states, "Open-ended questions offer children the opportunity to freely express feelings, motives and ideas." She states, "A question like "What color is that block?" evokes a one-word answer. But an open-ended question, "Tell me about the blocks you are using," encourages a child to describe the blocks or explain what he or she is doing. There is no right or wrong answer."[142]

Children have a lot to say most of the time, and it's important to listen attentively to their responses. This also gives adults the opportunity to extend the conversation, and to elicit more about the topic. This 'tell me more' is really important as a child is learning new words and building his vocabulary.

Here is a really interesting conversation that my preschoolers had one day about the existence of God. I asked open-ended questions to allow them to fully discuss their thoughts, and to share them with their classmates.

Child 1: *How did God make the people? Out of wood?*
Child 2: *I know. God made the world and it was empty. Then he created a boy and the boy said, "I'm so lonely." And one day he created a girl and that's it.*
Teacher: *What happens if someone doesn't believe in God?*
Child 2: *It's true. Really.*
Child 1: *You don't have to believe in God. It's okay but it's true that people are made from God.*
Child 3: *God is the king of everything and God doesn't like it when people exclude each other.*
Child 4: *God can punish you. He lives in the trees.*
Teacher: *Is God a "he" or a "she"?*
Child 4: *God is not a monkey. He's not a person. He's not an animal. God is right here.*

Teacher: Where?
Child 4: Yes. He is there and everywhere.
Teacher: I can't see him. How do I know he's there?
Child 4: You can't see him. I know he's there because. I know because I'm a paleontologist. I do things with science.
Teacher: You do a lot of things with science, like finding out about God? How many Gods are there?
Child 4: One
Teacher: So he lives in the trees and does what? What's the point of a God? Why do we have a God?
Child 4: He helps the earth grow.
Teacher: How does he do that?
Child 4: Nobody knows about God.
Teacher: If nobody knows, then how do you know?
Child 4: God is really mean.
Teacher: I thought he looks after you. How is he mean?
Child 4: He punishes people. God asks people to do good things. Sometimes he does bad things like punishes you.
Teacher: Does he give you a timeout?
Child 4: No. Punish means you can never become alive again. God's a teacher. He is everyone. God's not the bad guy in a fight. He fights people. He has a bow and arrow. He's the good guy. You can't see him. He's small. I will draw a picture of him. He has a triangle on his head. He used to be an old man who died.

Many of us, as parents, are tired of the one word, monosyllabic responses that children give when asked about their day in school, or what they played with. When asked, "What did you do in school today?" the standard response almost always is "Nothing." A 'tell-me-more' kind of question will elicit better responses. Lisa Wilkin states that if "…children only provide one-word responses to your open-ended questions, there are still ways you can encourage children to communicate more interactively."[143]

Problem solving in the sandbox

ONE DAY, I DECIDED TO spend some time watching the children play in the sandbox. The sandbox was equipped with many sand toys. In the center of the sandbox, there was a sensory table, which did not have a plug. As a result, the water flowed freely out of the water table. At the sandbox, I watched as a little boy patiently walked up to the sensory table and poured buckets of water into it. Then he stepped back and watched the water trickle down a hole. He then tried to plug the hole with sand. He saw me watching and said, "The water keeps going away into the hole." I asked him what his plan was to plug the hole. He said, "I keep putting sand, but the hole is still there." I didn't give him the answer but asked yet another question: "Is there anything else that you see in the sand box that might work to plug that hole?"

In a couple of minutes, I saw him run up to me with a plastic cup. "Yes!" he exclaimed. This will work!"…and it did!

Teachers in the preschool environment often use the Vygotskian approach of helping a child reach his/her zone of proximal development (ZPD), the area between a child's level of independent performance (what he/she can do alone) and the child's level of assisted performance (what he/she can do with support). Teachers use instructional strategies such as I did (which include hints, prompts, and cues) to scaffold the child's learning and development and to help him reach a new place in his understanding and development.[144]

"You'll never find a rainbow if you're looking down"
-Charles Chaplin

REFLECTIONS
ON TEACHING

"Education begins the gentleman, but reading, good company and reflection must finish him"

-John Locke

I see realization as the first step towards action. As author Paulo Freire says, "You need reflection and action upon the world in order to transform it." My decades of teaching experience have afforded me the time to reflect upon my practices, to discuss them with my colleagues, and to better understand child development both as a theory and as a practice. This section consists of my reflections, many centered on my trip to South Africa, where I worked with my colleague, Todd Hioki. Working with him in the villages of South Africa, and bouncing ideas off him, helped me better integrate the theory that we have read and learned about into our teaching practice.

CHAPTER 1

"One of the most difficult things is not to change society-but to change yourself!"

\- Nelson Mandela

On Developmentally Appropriate Practice

I ENDED MY WORK TRIP to South Africa with a visit to Robben Island. I wanted to get a feel of the great man that was Nelson Mandela. As I sat in the plane on my way home to Los Angeles, I knew definitively that the trip had changed me. Both Gandhi who said, "Be the change you wish to see in the world" and Mandela who said, "One of the most difficult things is not to change society, but to change yourself" were right. The six weeks in South Africa opened my eyes to the fact that being an educator is to be the change that we wish to see in the world and that change is changing the lives of children whose lives we can touch, either directly or indirectly.

Education for young children is their basic right, and teachers all over the world work towards helping them achieve their dreams through educating themselves (teachers). This means educating the 'Whole Child.' Many wonder what it really means to educate the 'Whole Child'. A 1930 report of the White House Conference on Children and Youth said this about the whole child: "To the doctor, the child is a typhoid patient; to the playground supervisor, a first baseman; to the teacher, a learner of arithmetic. At times, he may be different things to each of these specialists, but too rarely is he a whole child to any of them."[145] Simply stated, educating the 'Whole Child' means "attending to cognitive, social, emotional, physical, and talent development of children and youth from widely diverse backgrounds.

In order for children to learn, they need to be in a place where learning is possible, where the optimum conditions for survival are met; and these conditions are best met through adopting a 'Developmentally Appropriate Practice'.

Developmentally Appropriate Practice, often shortened to DAP, is an approach that is adopted by early childhood educators. It is grounded in the research and theories of how young children grow develop and learn.

The three core considerations of DAP are:

- Knowing about child development and learning.
- Knowing what is individually appropriate.
- Knowing what is culturally important.[146]

All areas of development and learning are important – we need to look at the 'Whole Child' in terms of physical, cognitive and social-emotional development of a child.

Children develop best when they have secure relationships. When we think of classrooms with 60 children aged 6 months and up, it's difficult to think that teachers and children are able to form those meaningful relationships that help children trust their caregivers. However, when caregivers give children the opportunity to learn through play, and when they engage in meaningful dialogue with children, children learn to form secure attachments and thrive in such environments.

It has been said that development and learning occur in and are influenced by multiple social and cultural contexts. Despite there being so much poverty in the villages that we visited, what is important to consider is that development happens in ALL social contexts. Yes, there are differences, and yes, there are shortcomings. However, given the right kind of classroom environment and caring and responsive teachers, children can develop and learn to their full potential.

Children learn in a variety of ways. Looking at learning through the lenses of Gardner's theory of Multiple Intelligences, one knows that children learn in a variety of ways. And so, arranging the classroom in a thoughtful way can help children learn in the way that best suits their individual style of learning.

Dr. Thomas Armstrong, an expert in the Theory of Multiple Intelligences, wrote, "The theory of multiple intelligences was developed in 1983 by Dr. Howard Gardner, professor of education at Harvard University. It suggests that the traditional notion of intelligence, based on I.Q. testing, is far too limited. Instead, Dr. Gardner proposes eight different intelligences to account for a broader range of human potential in children and adults.[147]

These intelligences are:
- Linguistic intelligence (word smart)
- Logical-mathematical intelligence (number/reasoning smart)
- Spatial intelligence (picture smart)
- Bodily-Kinesthetic intelligence (body smart)
- Musical intelligence (music smart)
- Interpersonal intelligence (people smart)
- Intrapersonal intelligence (self smart)
- Naturalist intelligence (nature smart)

Perhaps the most important point to consider is that children's experiences shape their motivation and approaches to learning. Therefore, giving children the opportunity to interact with materials that are both attractive and engaging, helps to motivate them to learn better and to enjoy their learning, through play.

As we educators work with children, being aware of DAP helps us plan curriculums and provide opportunities to develop and grow. And to open the doors to new learning.

"Our lives begin to end the day we become silent about things that matter."

-Martin Luther King, Jr.

CHAPTER 2

"Where have all the flowers gone...when will we ever learn?"
– Pete Seeger

On Rushing Children into Growing Up

RUSHING CHILDREN IS NOT A phenomenon that is exclusive to South Africa – it is a global problem. What we are doing to our young children is robbing them of their childhood – stealing from them their very right to play, laugh, run, jump, to be *children*. Today's children are being made to grow up way before their time. And that's alarming.

Our little ones under five years of age come to preschool to be children, not to be miniature adults. And yet, we rush them in that process of growing up. In fact, Friedrich Froebel, the founder of kindergarten, designed kindergarten to be 'a garden for children', a space for them to play and grow.

Today's kindergarten is akin to first grade, and first grade akin to second grade. Young children are exposed to the 'chalk and talk' method of teaching, or worse still, the 'skill and drill'. They have scant time to play; they sit on chairs and at desks, and in some countries, they lug heavy backpacks to preschool. So, where have all those flowers gone? How are we nurturing them?

According to Davis Elkind, psychologist and author, "The problem is snowballing. People are even trying to condition their babies in the womb now. At the infant level, there's the 'superbaby' phenomenon with flash cards at 3 months. An infant who can recognize flash cards is a monstrosity – it is a performance to please the parents and reflects the parents' need, not the child's. Then there's early reading, early math, early computers, early sports, early beauty contests... Parents have always had high hopes for their kids, but what's new is visiting on preschoolers the expectations and anxieties normally reserved for high school seniors."[148]

We have parents who buy 'Baby Einstein' books and DVDs or 'Baby Mozart' CDs with the hope of turning their little one into some kind of child prodigy. Before children have built the muscles to even hold a pencil, they are off taking lessons in piano or violin. According to Anne Stoudt, a kindergarten teacher, "While young students' reading and math scores are soaring, there is little assessment of the effect of the intensified academic focus on kids' motivation to learn, creativity, motor skills, social skills, or self-esteem. The risk is children who are already burned out on school by the time they reach third grade. Play is how children learn. There should be more of it in the upper grades, not less in the lower."[149] And while we are bemoaning the fact that preschool has become too academic, there is new research emerging about the importance of play in an adult's life.

More and more research suggests that healthy playtime leads to healthy adulthood. Childhood play is essential for brain development. According to Dr. Stuart Brown, we need to clearly define what play is. He says, "Play is something done for its own sake," he explains. "It's voluntary, it's pleasurable, it offers a sense of engagement, it takes you out of time. And the act itself is more important than the outcome."[150]

So it's time to bring out the Monopoly and the Checkers; dust off the Go board; bring out the Carrom Board and the marbles...and start playing. Let's give children back their childhood.

"Life is more fun if you play games."
-Roald Dahl

CHAPTER 3

"A curriculum is only as good as its context."

A Fresh Look At Curriculum

THE PRINCIPALS OF THE SCHOOLS we visited in South Africa reached out to us asking for help with planning curriculum. All preschools in the area have what is commonly referred to as 'canned curriculum'– curriculum that is preplanned and has a set theme each week. This works, at least to an extent.

My own learning began the minute I stepped out of the car, into the villages that I was visiting. I had to closely examine my own values of honoring emergent curriculum.

Emergent curriculum, the brainchild of Elizabeth Jones, "is a constructive curriculum in which the teachers, students, teaching materials and environment interact in the context of dialogue. It departs away from the idea "everything is predefined" and maintains that "everything is developing". Curriculum activity, instead of pure cognitive activity, is the dynamic process in which teachers and students display and create the significance of the life."[151]

Steeped in my own cultural biases and opinions, I planned the curricula for the teachers' workshops. Ironically, I had brought my very own version of 'canned curriculum'– PowerPoint presentations and lesson plans of what I would do in a classroom of teachers, none of whom I had ever met. I had an open mind about what could be changed; however, in a way, my mind was closed, because I thought I knew what to teach.

We had planned a lot of activities centered around water play. Water play is good for children's physical, cognitive and social-emotional development. Sensory play of this sort is open ended: there is no right or wrong play with water. It lends itself to thousands of possibilities, and all children can be successful at this activity.

Free play with water can build the foundation for understanding

- physics (flow, motion),
- chemistry (solutions, cohesion),
- biology (plant and animal life), and
- mathematics (measurement, equivalence, volume).

Mastery of these concepts will support children's understanding of academic subjects in later schooling and life. Science is indeed "serious play." Science is everywhere around us. What can children do to increase their understanding of science? Everything! Children inquire, observe, compare, imagine, invent, design experiments, and theorize when they explore natural science materials such as water, sand, and mud.

Through water play, children learn about concepts like

- empty/full,
- before/after,
- shallow/deep,
- heavy/light
- Float
- Strain[152]

As we were driving to the villages near Kruger National Park, I had my first "a-ha" moment. It was not going to work! We had bought enormous bags of cornstarch for sensory play and goop. Big problem: there's no water to make the goop; and there's no water to wash it off either. We had brought scoops for sand play: again, big mistake: when sand gets in the hair of children, they have serious problems. Again, not going to work. As I went down the list, more and more of the agenda items moved from the agenda list to the trash list.

So, we created sensory bottles with colored water and tiny animals for the teachers, and scuttled our plans of goop, water and sand. We made piles of soft pliable play dough, knowing that teachers would love it. But we created all of this without ever interacting with teachers.

Why was this also a mistake? Because it still did not take into account the fact that it is through experience that children understand the meaning of the curriculum. We already know that children do not learn through rote and it is through hands-on experience that the learning gets a context. Put simply by Zhang Zeng-tian and Jin Yu-le, "Emergent curriculum manifests the deep level understanding of the curriculum."[153]

That sent us right back to the drawing board. I knew that we had to understand the culture of the villages that we were in and the cultural values and experiences of the teachers we were meeting before we could train them on curriculum. I have emphasized above that a curriculum is only as good as its context. Then how could we teach the importance of block play, when children had merely three blocks to manipulate? How could we stress the importance of having more dramatic play for boys when all they had to play with were a couple of broken plastic cars with only three wheels each?

My learning came slowly: I realized that in order to train teachers about the importance of such materials for young children, those very materials need to *be* in the classroom –

if not in abundance, then at least enough for a few children to engage with.

We visited schools and took account of what the teachers' schedules looked like; we spent time with children to see how the long day stretched before them with no toys to interact with. To the outsider, it was terrible that there was not much happening in terms of curriculum. But, then we had realized how debilitating poverty can be.

During the visits, I also realized that there were often too many children for a teacher to manage, but restating the problem wasn't going to be helpful. I had to strategize and come up with ideas that would work: creating learning spaces, pockets and islands that needed teacher scaffolding, as well as other spaces where children did not need the guidance of a teacher. While I worked on this, my colleague, Todd, steadfastly created toys for the classroom and through the creation and building of those valuable toys, he helped the teachers explore the power of their own creations.

The classrooms now had toys. They had tables and shelves thanks to Teacher Todd's amazing creativity. And slowly, as though we were building a house brick by brick, the teachers and Todd and I constructed a new knowledge and a new, solid curriculum. It emerged through our observation of the teachers, and the interplay between strategy and creation. A curriculum that was culture-centered and need-based. That grew from the rich conversations that we had with the teachers, and from our close interaction with the children and their environment. A curriculum that continued to be pre-planned, but now, had elements of emergent curriculum and child development needs in it. It was a curriculum that respected and valued not just the children, but also the teachers, and their learning – a curriculum that had its foundation in play.

"Don't limit a child to your own learning, for he was born in another time."

-Rabindranath Tagore

CHAPTER 4

"I became a teacher because I wanted revenge – I wanted to beat children like I was beaten..."

Conversations about Reflective Teaching

OUR TWO-WEEK TRAINING/MENTORING IN THE villages culminated on a Saturday with a teacher workshop. We decided to focus on teacher reflections: Why do we teach? How do we teach? What frustrates us? And, how can we do things differently? We had asked them these questions at the beginning of the workshop, and decided to do a little in-depth soul searching at the end.

We role played. One of the teachers was the 'teacher' while the others were children in the classroom. We asked the teachers to set up activities for the children and then engage them in play.

As we discussed the process of teacher engagement, we elicited responses from both the 'teachers' and the 'children'. What made the class easier to teach? What made it more difficult? What made it interesting? The responses were illustrative of the journey that we had been through with them: the journey of understanding the role of constructivism in a teacher/ learner's life.

The constructivist perspective of readiness and development was advanced by theorists such as Jean Piaget, Maria Montessori, and Lev Vygotsky. Although their work varies greatly, each articulates a similar context of learning and development. They believe that "learning and development occur when young children interact with the environment and people around them." Constructivists view young children as "active participants in the learning process." In addition, constructivists believe that young children initiate most of the activities required for learning and development.[154]

John Dewey "proposed a method of "directed living" where students would engage in real-world, practical workshops in which they would demonstrate their knowledge through creativity and collaboration."[155] In his opinion, students should be provided with opportunities to think for themselves and articulate their thoughts.

The teachers were really excited with the role play: They realized that it was far easier to manage children when children were sitting, as opposed to when they were standing; that in order for teachers to engage with children, the following should happen:

- Teachers should be well planned.
- Children should have choices.
- Teachers should have activity plans.
- All domains of development should be addressed.
- Hands-on activities are a necessary component of a preschool classroom.
- Teachers should greet their children warmly and make them feel welcome.

Through the process of role play and dialogue, we all decided that the best way to learn was through a hands-on approach. Our workshop and training seemed to take on the philosophy of constructivism, As Dewey said, "Give the pupils something to do, not something to learn; and the doing is of such a nature as to demand thinking; learning naturally results."[156]

So Teacher Todd and I set up hands-on activities for the teachers to do – and not just any kind of hands-on. These were activities that resulted in the teachers creating resources for their classroom. Activities that catapulted them into the role of builder, carpenter, and creator.

They enjoyed using the hammers and drills, and were really comfortable with the staple gun. In a couple of hours, they had fashioned little wooden cars (made from blocks of wood and washers), wooden blocks to play with, and fabric covered table tops for activity centers!

Arthur Chickering and Stephen C. Ehrmann wrote, "Learning is not a spectator sport. Students do not learn much just sitting in classes listening to teachers, memorizing prepackaged assignments, and spitting out answers. They must talk about what they are learning, write reflectively about it, relate it to past experiences, and apply it to their daily lives. They must make what they learn part of themselves."[157] Thus, at the end of the workshop, when we asked teachers to reflect on the learning process over the past week, they wrote about how they transformed as teachers. One of them who had shared with us that she became a teacher to "beat children as she had been beaten" wrote how she wanted to greet children with a smile even when she was in a bad mood. And all of them reflected on how much they had learned through the construction of blocks, tables and toys. They wrote that they value play and never realized how learning was embedded in play. And they all wrote about the fun they had.

"Learning is finding out what you already know. Doing is demonstrating that you know it. Teaching is reminding others that they know just as well as you. You are all learners, doers, teachers."

-Richard Bach

CHAPTER 5

"The children are playing...as if the teachers do not exist"

The Philosophy of Montessori, Piaget and Vygotsky

AS TEACHERS, WE OFTEN ASK of ourselves, "Did we have a measure of success today?" On one such occasion, as I reminisced about our day, I think we did. In my opinion, on that day, we were teachers who showed cultural intelligence in the classroom.

We had gone to the schools in the South African villages thinking of all the great philosophers like Piaget, and Montessori and Vygotsky. But soon we realized that what we needed to do was take what would work from their teachings and adapt it to the culture we were in. So we took the 'exploration and discovery' from Piaget's teachings in order to set up the classroom.

Jean Piaget considered that "play is vitally related to cognitive development as it helps children construct knowledge and make sense of their world." Piaget promoted inquiry-based learning that focused on children as active learners in their environment, and included activities that are child-directed, and child-centered.[158]

Albert Einstein stated, "I am neither very clever nor especially gifted. I am only very, very curious!" It is this curiosity that teachers help foster by creating an environment that is ripe for exploration. The author of '*The Irresistible Classroom*' confirms this by stating that "children are naturally eager to learn about the world and everything in it.

When their interest is engaged, they push the boundaries of their knowledge, hungry for more."[159]

Then we looked at the materials that Maria Montessori created and thought of how they might be used in classrooms with many children and just one teacher. Maria Montessori developed and designed mathematically precise materials that are now known as Montessori materials. All Montessori materials follow six basic principles: meaningfulness to the child, the isolation of the difficulty in a single material, materials progress from simple to complex, materials prepare indirectly for future learning, and materials begin as concrete expressions and graduate to abstract. Additionally, Montessori materials are divided into four categories: practical life, sensorial, academic and cultural/artistic materials. Typically speaking, each Montessori material teaches just one skill or concept at a time.[160]

And then based on our observation of the struggle that the teachers and the children had with engagement, both socially and with toys, we thought of Vygotsky and scaffolding.

The notion of scaffolding has been linked to the work of psychologist Lev Vygotsky. He emphasized the role of social interaction as being crucial to cognitive development, so that learning first occurs at the social level. Thus, when a child (or a novice) learns with an adult or a more capable peer, the learning occurs within the child's zone of proximal development (ZPD). ZPD is defined as the "distance between the child's actual developmental level as determined by independent problem solving and the higher level of potential development as determined through problem solving under adult guidance and in collaboration with more capable peers". Enabling the learner to bridge this gap between the actual and the potential depends on the resources or the kind of support that is provided.[161]

A Kaleidoscope of Children

We set up the classroom with all the material at the children's level, where the children could play and interact with it comfortably. We encouraged the teachers to bring in the children in small groups so that we could help them learn to engage. At first, we saw hesitant and shy children come in to the room. They interacted with the material only when asked to or when shown how to. Slowly they warmed up, and then suddenly, it was as though a dam had burst. A dam of creativity, a dam of curiosity, a dam of fun, a dam of chatter…a dam of learning!

They built high towers and low walls; they fed their babies and cooked warm meals; they drove cars around, making 'car sounds'; they played make believe with the crocodiles; they cut and they colored; they glued and they read. They played!

"Education is the most powerful weapon which you can use to change the world."

-Nelson Mandela

CHAPTER 6

Getting from "uh-huh" to "A-ha!"- What does it take?

On the Need for an Environment Set Up for Exploration

BASED ON OUR OBSERVATIONS OF the school visits, Teacher Todd and I discussed strategies that might work in the classroom. We realized that children don't have enough manipulatives: there were still unopened boxes of puzzles on the shelves. What that told us was that we needed to give them objects to manipulate that had some kind of cultural relevance or familiarity.

We also realized that for the past many years, we have spoken about the use of 'centers', but that really had no meaning or context for them; hence, they didn't set up activities in centers. A "Learning Center" is an area "set up within the classroom each with a specific focus that encourages children to participate in the focus of that area. The purpose or goal of an Interest Center is to allow children to learn in the way they learn best: through play!"[162]

Thus, when we walked into the classrooms, we saw the few toys that the children had lying on the floor. The children stepped on the blocks, walked past them, and in some cases, even accidentally kicked them. That was when we had our "a-ha" moment! We needed to actually create centers and arrange toys/manipulatives in those centers so that teachers could see what we meant when we talked about child-centered activities, or curriculum set up based on the interests of the children. We also needed children to

185

understand boundaries for their activities in terms of space. And we needed to create an aesthetic surrounding; one that would excite and motivate, one that would pique the children's interest.

This posed a bit of a problem: the preschool classroom had neither chairs nor tables. The children just milled around during their 'free play' time. We began to think, "What does play mean to them?"

So Todd and I made yet another trip to the store. We bought wood and saws, paint and turpentine, drill bits and screws. We bought brooms and got them chopped down to child sized ones. Then we went to a bazaar near the bus stop to Mozambique – it was a riot of color, with every imaginable thing available. We bought fabric and buttons, mosquito netting and needles, and came back home with a very full car.

We repurposed plastic bottles, plastic trays, and created amazing things from scrap: small low tables, crayon and scissor holders, a storyboard to facilitate imaginative storytelling, and at least 400 blocks.

The next morning, we returned to the classrooms, laden with bags and packages. Then we set up the room methodically, and waited till the teachers came in to see the setup. They walked in and stared silently at everything. The principal of the preschool began to sob quietly. The teachers milled around excitedly, and then brought the children in to see the classroom. A hushed silence surrounded us, and they children filed in, google eyed and awed. Then, as they began to play, there was a pleasant hum in the room, and soon the classroom was filled with excited chatter and laughter.

Nothing was more exciting than watching the teachers and the children go from "uh-huh" to "a-ha!"

"The world is full of magic things, patiently waiting for our senses to grow sharper."

-W. B. Yeats

CHAPTER 7

Observing children at play – how do we observe 87 of them?

Classroom Arrangement and Classroom Management

Since I live and work in the United States, I tend to compare preschool arrangement and management in other countries with western counterparts. This doesn't always make sense, since the rules and policies differ not just from country to country, but also from state to state.

While in South Africa, Todd and I had to present workshops to the teachers working with preschool children in the villages. We were to start our on-site observations of children in the preschools (they call them crèches in South Africa and in India).

While we both had a lot of experience observing children (primarily in the United States) the task before us was quite daunting. Each classroom had between 50-85 children and one adult. The average classroom size was 250-300 sq. feet. To put this in perspective for our US minds, the California Title 22 (State Licensing for preschools and daycares) indoor space requirement PER child is 35 sq. feet. If we divide 300 by 35, we get 8.57: We can have only 8-9 children in that space, while here we had upwards of 50.

In India, preschool education is provided by private schools and government ICDS (Anganwadi) centers.

Each year, educators from the Teach with Africa Organization visit South Africa with a view to assist them in their curriculum planning. In the past, during these workshops other teachers had given them advice on classroom arrangement. So they had arranged their classrooms in curriculum or interest centers. And because of the shortage of space, their centers were pushed to the walls so that children could occupy the space in the middle.

We were in a quandary: We were focusing our energies on a combination of classroom arrangement and classroom management: this was new for the teachers. How could we really help with classroom management? The teachers in South Africa complained of the same problems that we complain of in the United States – the children were hitting each other; they weren't listening to the teacher; they were crying the whole day. Most importantly: they were not able to learn.

As educators, we need to pay attention to creating an environment that is conducive to learning. It's hard to learn in a class crammed with 50 other children, squashed like sardines. It's difficult trying to learn to share when the items to share are so few. It's almost impossible to learn when your basic needs are not met.

According to UNICEF, all children have rights.[163] They have the right to:

1. Be cared for
2. Protection
3. Participation
4. Freedom of expression
5. Education and Play
6. Survival and Development
7. Rehabilitation and Care

When children (all over the world, whether in India, South Africa or the United States) do not have their needs met, they are not in a position to learn, thrive and grow.

When we look at readiness to learn, we must first look at the environment that the child is in. The National Association for the Education of Young Children (1995) discusses this in the <u>NAEYC Position Statement on School Readiness</u>. This NAEYC statement underscores the fact that the environment is the 'third teacher'.

"The traditional construct of readiness unduly places the burden of proof on the child. Until the inequities of life experiences are addressed, the use of readiness criteria for determining school entry or placement blames children for their lack of opportunity. Furthermore, many of the criteria now used to assess readiness are based on inappropriate expectations of children's abilities and fail to recognize normal variation in the rate and nature of individual development and learning. NAEYC believes it is the responsibility of the schools to meet the needs of children as they enter school and to provide whatever services are needed in the least restrictive environment to help each child reach his or her fullest potential."[164]

So both Todd and I planned to spend the next few weeks trying to help create an environment that makes it possible for children to learn (within the space/number limitations that the schools had). We then intended to spend another week analyzing our observations in order to understand what to base our next workshop on.

Lighting fires in the preschool classroom

IT WAS AMAZING TO SEE how the process of engagement had worked. We saw it in terms of children learning to engage with material and in terms of teachers learning to engage with children. It was like Plutarch said, "The mind is not a vessel to be filled, but a fire to be kindled."

When we visited the schools in the last week, we realized that the biggest problem wasn't the shortage of funds or material. What we saw instead was the need for a spark to be lit – a spark of excitement, a spark of enthusiasm, a spark of engagement with materials and people.

Teacher Todd and I spent the week trying to strategize how to kindle that excitement in the classroom. The general morale was low; there were too many children in one classroom with a single teacher. We decided to try and work with the following:

- Help the teachers create material, and help them feel self- sufficient
- Help them learn to engage with children, and
- Help children learn to engage with materials.

We worked with the teachers at the school, primarily with one of them. We showed him ways of becoming an intentional teacher while planning his setup of the curriculum. Teachers must be 'intentional' in their planning for play. Author Marilyn Rice, in her article, *'What is the teacher's role in supporting play in early childhood classrooms?'* throws light on this topic. She states that planning should not be accidental – "It just happened..." On the contrary, she stresses that "...it should be something that the teacher planned and intended." According to Marilyn Rice, "play serves several functions in contributing to children's social and emotional development when they assume new roles that require new social skills, and take the perspectives of their peers."[165]

The teacher we had been mentoring had been working on arranging the classroom with intentionality. The activities were set up on low tables. They were organized in a manner that had aesthetic appeal. Our ideas for the setup of activities were inspired by the Reggio Emilia philosophy of using 'provocations'. Provocations are "deliberate and thoughtful decisions made by the teacher to extend the ideas of children.

Teachers provide materials, media and general direction as needed but the children take the ideas where they want."[166]

When teachers set up activities in a manner that provokes curiosity, children are inspired to play and learn. This was so evident on that day when the children walked in to the classroom, and stopped short. One could hear them gasp, see their eyes widen as they took in everything. It certainly was a sight to behold. The children still needed to be coaxed and encouraged to try activities, but once they had warmed up, their eyes lit up and the room was filled with their infectious laughter. Play and learning should be integrated throughout the day. And the facilitation will be the most effective if it is complemented by a carefully planned classroom environment.

"A mind that is learning never says, 'I know,' because knowledge is always partial, whereas learning is complete all the time. Learning does not mean starting with a certain amount of knowledge, and adding to it further knowledge. That is not learning at all; it is a purely mechanistic process. To me, learning is something entirely different. I am learning about myself from moment to moment, and the myself is extraordinarily vital; it is living, moving; it has no beginning and no end. When I say, 'I know myself,' learning has come to an end in accumulated knowledge. Learning is never cumulative; it is a movement of knowing which has no beginning and no end."
-J. Krishnamurti, *The Book of Life*

CHAPTER 8

"We don't stop playing because we grow old; we grow old because we stop playing."

-George Bernard Shaw

Reflections From a Hands-on Workshop

IT WAS THE LAST DAY of our 3-day workshop. We decided to focus on large motor activities and the importance of play in the morning, and we had a really good time.

We tried to use what was already in the environment – we strung up thick yarn to create a kind of spider's web that we had to step over and under. We put the hula hoops on the ground so that we had to cross the river that was full of crocodiles (the hula hoops were our islands!). Then we walked down a very bumpy path (using old tires that they had, laid out around a patch of grass). And then, we crept down a very narrow path (a balance beam that Todd created) and found the lion. There was a lot of slipping and sliding, squealing and laughing, and running and tripping – a great workout before breakfast.

Todd and I had been trying to give the teachers ideas about large motor activities that can be done in large groups, because as I said before, each teacher had 70-85 children in their care.

Todd brought in some saws for the teachers to create blocks with. We wanted to include creativity and woodworking in the activities of the day. While the morning was spent building overall large body muscles, we decided to include sawing as an activity to strengthen the upper arm and shoulder muscles. The teachers tried their hands at sawing, and also at using other simple tools: drills and screw drivers. While engaged in this large and small muscle activity, the teachers created small toys and blocks for themselves.

We closed the workshop with a hands-on activity of creating objects from materials meant for recycling. We asked them to focus on the three domains of development and to create an object which could answer these questions:

- What have you made?
- Why do you think this is going to be helpful for children?
- What domain of development will this help with?
- How will you assess their participation in the activity?

The teachers were wonderfully creative, and the results we got were excellent. They created puzzles from foam meat trays, and dolls to explain the parts of the body using paper plates and paper fasteners. The doll even had egg carton boots!

We couldn't wait to visit their schools from Monday onward. We knew that there would be so much for us to share and learn. We created a 'tree of learning' that had its foundation in play. The teachers added post-it leaves with ideas of things that they have learned from us. Todd and I were planning on spending the next week observing them, and I was sure that we too would have our oak leaves of learning to add to the tree.

We had set up the classroom like a preschool classroom – with manipulatives, blocks, small motor activities, art and sensory activities. We had made our own play dough, finger paint and glue. While I found that they were eager to play with the play dough, most of them were reluctant to get into the sensory activities. They stayed away from the paint and the glue. Since we wanted to be sensitive to their culture, we didn't have a water table – water is a scarcity here, and it obviously would not have been a good idea. (A water table is nothing but a large plastic container, usually on a frame, that is used for sensory activities in a preschool environment)

The teachers we worked with loved music. When they began singing, they would sound like a church choir. Their beautiful voices would harmonize. We played hopscotch and a home-made version of twister – we used hula hoops and paper shapes. It was a lot of fun, and the teachers really got into it.

The problems these teachers face are so severe that I don't think that we can wrap our minds around them. Each of them has around 80 children that he/she single-handedly has to manage. And if that isn't enough, they have to double up as administrative staff on an as-needed basis.

The problem of overcrowding of preschool classrooms is prevalent in India too. Anganwadi preschools in India are only 250-300 square feet and have 25 children in each class.

The Ministry of Women and Child Development (MWCD) plays a central role in Early Childhood Care and Education (ECCE) activities in India. Since 1975, the MWCD has been providing free-of-charge integrated child development services (ICDS) in the areas of health, nutrition, and education to children in rural areas, minority groups, slums, and underdeveloped areas through these ECCE centers called Anganwadi (meaning "courtyard shelter" in Hindi). By 2011, about 38 million people participated in ICDS education programs, and about 78 million people took part in health and nutrition programs at Anganwadi centers (MWCD, 2011), the largest numbers in the world.[167]

We spent the afternoon strategizing ways to manage large groups, both indoors and outdoors. I suggested that the teachers try to set up the environments in three different ways:free play, self-directed play and teacher-directed play. This day of teacher activities and play was intended as a precursor to the real thing: the teachers went back to their classrooms to set them up in meaningful ways, based on the ideas that they had got from the workshop.

The day was long; it was exhausting; the day was fun! We had a great time working in the classrooms. We created toys; we worked with our hands; and we learned so much. As we played, we hoped to discover the child in each one of us.

"Adults are just outdated children."

-Dr. Seuss

CHAPTER 9

Make Books Come Alive!

On the Need for Props to Move Children from Receptive to Productive Language

I WAS RAISED IN INDIA at a time when materials were scarce and money was hard to come by. I grew up as part of an extended family of ten children. Since I was the youngest, I survived on hand-me-downs, both toys and clothes. The ones that I most looked forward to were the well-thumbed books of my older siblings and cousins.

As children, we were surrounded by books and so grew up with a profound love for literature. Shakespeare rubbed shoulders with Enid Blyton on our shelves. Space was scarce in our home, and yet every shelf and corner was crammed with books. Every time we wanted an imaginative getaway, a book was always available. I remember reading Robert Louis Stevenson's 'Land of Counterpane', shutting my eyes and traveling through vast dark skies into an enchanted world where animals could talk or fly, and witches mixed bubbling potions.

Inspired by such imagery, I tried mixing potions of my own in glass Coke bottles, using residual cola and talcum powder (borrowed from my mother's cabinet). I'd stir frantically to produce a white foam. Little did I know, at the tender age of five, that I was instinctively 'curriculum webbing' the stories I'd read into a self-devised chemistry experiment.

From those early experiences stemmed a longing to work with children, to infuse in them a love for literature and help integrate all their 'multiple intelligences'. I realized that through a 'whole language' approach, I could 'web' different areas of curriculum, basing them on books and literature.

Dr. Monica Bomengen describes this process in the simplest terms possible. She states "…the 'whole language approach' is a method of teaching children to read by recognizing words as whole pieces of language." Dr. Bomengen adds that proponents of the whole language philosophy believe that language should not be broken down into letters and combinations of letters and "decoded." "Instead", she says, "they believe that language is a complete system of making meaning, with words functioning in relation to each other in context."[168] Unfortunately, teachers around the world have very tight budgets on which to manage their curriculum – they have to buy a lot of their own school supplies and materials. Despite the good intentions of every early child educator, a teacher rarely uses props when reading to young children. Materials are expensive and often not easily available.

Why buy when you can make?

A FEW YEARS AGO, ON a long flight from San Francisco to Philadelphia, I was seated next to a doctor. We chatted for a while and I found out that she was a specialist in Alzheimer's disease. Curious to learn how to avoid the dreaded disease, I asked her what I could do. "Just create. Keep that brain alive: Get those neurons working!" Those words keep echoing in my mind as I look dismally at today's consumer society.

I lived in an era and in a country where handwork was highly encouraged. I had several dolls and all the furniture in my doll house was made from old match boxes. My doll house even had a Styrofoam toilet! Granted, it didn't look like the lovely little plastic ones that you get today. However, it was created by me.

And that is the important point that we all seem to be losing focus of: creating things. Why create when you could probably buy it somewhere, sometimes ironically even cheaper than it costs to produce it? The answer lies in a process of self-discovery. Creation is an experience that is incomparable, whether one is talking about a child creating or an adult doing so. The simple act of creation can give one a rush of adrenalin; much like that one gets after completing a marathon.

It is important for adults to literally go back to the drawing board, look for inspiration and create tools and props to help children read, because in reality, that process of creating props leads to the creation of something (someone) far bigger: an accomplished reader.

Theorists have established the link between the use of props in literature and the reading ability of children. It is extremely important for adults to pay careful attention to acquiring or making props to move children to the next level of language competency, i.e. reading. In the chapters that ensue, I set out some case studies that show how useful props and puppets are as literacy aids.

"Fill your house with stacks of books, in all the crannies and all the nooks."

-Dr. Seuss

CHAPTER 10

"Puppets allow for children's visions and inspirations to come to life."

-Carina Cancelli, Montessori Teacher

The Importance of Using Glove Puppets and Finger Puppets

THE USE OF PROPS IN literacy development has been highlighted by several experts. Authors Raines & Isbell stress on the importance of the role of storytelling in a child's life. According to them, "Storytelling is a powerful medium. A well-told story can inspire action, foster cultural appreciation, expand children's knowledge, or provide sheer enjoyment. Listening to stories helps children understand their world and how people relate to each other in it." Raines states, that a story told by the teacher and retold by children is a powerful literacy tool for the early childhood classroom. "Storytelling," she adds, "provides a pleasurable literacy connection that has the power to positively impact children's attitudes toward stories throughout their lives."[169]

Empirical studies of children's story comprehension tell us that children learn to comprehend stories when they integrate what they hear when read to, with their own sensory perceptions.[170] This view of the importance of the need for a language-rich environment has overwhelming support. Vivian Paley agrees with this view, adding that children transcribe and expose the words and images that

199

crowd their minds and place them on a stage, becoming actor, writer, critic, linguist, mathematician, and philosopher all at once.[171]

It is with the use of puppets, props and other teaching aids that a teacher can help a child transform and change his world into a new one, one that is rich in literacy experience.

TRUE STORIES

a. "My child doesn't read..."

CHILDREN BEGIN THEIR LITERACY EXPERIENCES by listening as stories are read aloud first by parents, grandparents and teachers. Then they start to read those stories by themselves. The next stage of reading involves the retelling of the stories where they use puppets and props to dramatize and role play favorite stories.

It is very important to understand this sequence. Since receptive language comes before productive language, immersing a child in an environment where stories are read to them is very important. As a child grows from receptive to productive language, the environment should be rich in props that will encourage language production, i.e. productive language. Joseph Lao, in his article on language acquisition makes a clear distinction between receptive and productive language. He states that "receptive speech refers to speech that is understood. Productive speech refers to speech that is produced." He elaborates on this by stating that our ability to recognize sounds and words tends to exceed our ability to actually produce those sounds and words. "As a result, infants tend to understand verbal communications better than they can produce them."[172]

Vivian Paley supports this view, adding, "In the telling and performing of stories, all ideas must be heard, considered, compared, interpreted and acted upon. The bridges built in play are lengthened, their partially exposed signposts organized and labeled in ways that commit the storyteller to travel in particular directions. The subject encompasses all of language and thought." When adults pay careful attention to the process of language acquisition, they can help children grow from eager participants in storytelling sessions to powerful and capable writers.

Puppets

- Help resolve conflicts
- Increase language competency
- Deal with emotions like fear and inadequacy

Children have always been delighted by puppets. Cultures from all over the world have had puppet shows and stories told in puppet form. Ancient literature and stories were often dramatized as puppet shows and these shows were attended by both old and young. Theory has shown that children respond well to the use of puppetry especially when they are scared or frightened. Puppets have been used by adults to solve emotional problems and to encourage the production of speech.

It is both sad and ironic that with the invention of the television, adults have resorted to using animated puppet shows and have gone away from traditional string puppets and the like.

Puppets can range from simple stick puppets to complicated 'jack-in-the-box' kinds of puppets. All of the materials used in the making of these puppets are relatively inexpensive and can be made in a short amount of time.

Stick Puppets:

Since stick puppets involve the use of one hand, try and pick stories that have no more than two characters. It is very difficult for young children to change puppets quickly while attempting to re-enact or re-tell a story.

Finger Puppets:

When using finger puppets in the telling of a story, make sure that the puppets don't exceed the fingers of one hand (i.e. five) Choose stories and songs that involve numbers (one to five) Encouraging children to use finger puppets in the counting of one to five and backwards from five to one introduces early mathematical concepts of one-to one-correspondence. Avoid using finger puppets in stories where you need to change characters frequently. Children find it extremely difficult to participate in finger plays and stories when they have to pay attention to many characters.

b. Using puppets to learn language

WORKING IN THE UNITED STATES where there is so much diversity sometimes brings one in contact with children who know no English. Such was the case with Gregorio. Straight off a plane from South America, he was here to attend preschool. He understood not one word of English and chose to retreat into a shell and keep quiet for the entire eight hour period that he was with us.

We tried in vain to make conversation with him, but he was fast retreating into his shell. I fished into my pocket and brought out five frog puppets. He turned to push me away but then stopped, his eyes riveted on the frog puppets. He watched mesmerized as I slowly slid each puppet onto my fingers. I kept my eyes on him, and slowly began to sing, "Five green and speckled frogs…" He said nothing and watched till the song was complete. Then he turned around and played on his own till his parent picked him up.

The next day, he returned to his solitary self, interacting with no one. Once again, I approached him, and brought out the puppets. This time, he turned and positioned his body so he could see me properly. There was a glimmer of a smile as he watched me sing the song. Then as he did the day before, he turned away from me and continued to play with the blocks. I took the puppets off my fingers and placed them on the floor near him. Then I stood up and left him to play on his own, observing him from a distance. He looked around, saw that he was alone, then put the puppets on his own fingers. He began to sing the song: it did not sound like the song that I had just sung. However, he was in tune, moving his fingers and removing the puppets one at a time, till he reached the number zero.

The day after, Gregorio did something totally different: He ran up to me, held my hand and said, "Frog." I smiled at him and the two of us went to look for the frog puppets. From then on, he could be seen humming and singing on his own, mastering the songs and finger plays till he was ready to practice his English with the rest of the class. That is now history. He is now in the first grade, speaking nineteen to the dozen. Little does he know what an important role the frog puppets played in his life.

c. Using flannel pieces to encourage language production

ENGLISH, AS WE KNOW IT, is not the first language of many children; therefore, it is not surprising that several preschoolers come into a school setting with little or no English. When teachers read stories to children, they tend to forget that simple fact: He doesn't understand English. The little child sits at circle for a bit, and then, after a short while, loses interest and then wanders off to find something else to do.

Such was the case with Rani. I was a director in a preschool in Pune, and Rani was a student at the school. She spoke only Hindi. However, the story sessions were only in English. "We are an English–medium school…" we would proudly proclaim, ignoring the fact that most of the children attending the school were in fact, first generation English learners.

Rani would come in and listen to the story for a couple of minutes. Then, she would begin to pull at her socks, and then start fidgeting. After a few minutes of restless behavior, she would try and wander away from the group. The teachers would try, in vain to attract her attention.

The teachers would plan diligently and read out aloud stories about animals and dragons, sure that the children would be riveted to their stories. However, when a child does not understand what you are saying nor has any context to understand the language with, you may as well be speaking in Greek.

After observing Rani for a couple of weeks, I asked the teachers to try and use flannel board stories to make the stories more visually appealing; more importantly, to give the children the ability to play with the characters and re-tell the story. They agreed and began to tell simple stories that were cumulative in nature, where new characters were added as each page was turned. Then after story time, the book and the flannel pieces were left for the children to interact with.

We watched as Rani began to get engaged with story time. She would crawl under the table and peek at the story surreptitiously. Then once the session was over, she would walk up to the flannel board, and place the pieces one at a time on the flannel board, all the while saying nothing.

This continued for a couple of weeks. Every single day, for those two weeks, we repeated the same story (till some of the children actually began to say "not that story!"). The new day dawned, and like clockwork, Rani went over to the flannel board. She picked up the pieces and began to place them on the board in sequence. This time, I could hear hushed words. Rani had actually memorized the story and was practicing it by herself. Rani learned English in her own quiet way, and till she was at preschool, she could be found interacting with the books and the flannel characters.

d. Using puppets to express emotions

WHEN CHILDREN ARE YOUNG, UNDER the age of five, adults know and expect them to have temper tantrums and throw fits. However, what adults fail to understand is all of the emotional upheaval that a preschooler faces, and the big job he has of forming his ego. It's a delicate dance for a young child, learning how to balance ego, moods and self-esteem. Throw into that mix a healthy portion of related or unrelated problems: other preschoolers who have the same issues, sibling rivalry, language problems, etc.

It is no wonder then that many preschoolers who do not know how to express anger or frustration, then resort to what adults refer to as 'bad behavior', and are admonished for it. Adults quickly brush aside children's feelings and expect the young preschoolers to behave normally, never allowing them to really vent their feeling.

Such was the case of Emilia. She would come into school proudly proclaiming each toy to be "mine" and would scream loudly if anyone came within a mile of those toys. Emilia was all of 3-and-a-half. She was sandwiched between an older and a younger sibling. She was often both the bully and the bullied, resorting to taking toys away from her infant sister.

She came into school crying one sunny morning, proclaiming that she was mad. She stomped around the room, refusing to play with toys or friends, preferring instead to sit on the chair and cry. When asked what had happened, her parent brushed it off, saying that Emilia had had a rough morning.

At circle, I brought out the happy face and sad face zebra puppet that I had. We went round the circle describing our moods to the class. When it was Emilia's turn, she refused to say anything and turned away from the class. Then, suddenly, she ran up to me, took the puppet and said, "The zebra is mad. Not Emilia. The zebra is mad. Zebra's mommy is mad and zebra has no toys because baby took away all zebra's toys." She said this in one long breath, threw the puppet down and flounced off. After circle was over, I went up to Emilia and we spoke at length about how zebra felt about the whole situation and we problem solved about what we could do to make zebra feel better. All along, we teachers knew that zebra was none other than Emilia and that she needed the puppet to give vent to her true feelings of frustration and anger.

Julia Luckenbill, in her article on circle time has this to say about the importance of puppets: "Using persona puppets to talk with children about their problems is the most valuable tool in my bag of teaching tricks. The puppets are so good at helping children get along! Puppets allow young children to think about solutions to conflicts and are a great way for children to explore their feelings. Children who talk about different points of view with props like puppets often have an easier time getting along with others and making friends. Puppets can also support anti-bias curriculum efforts and introduce feeling words, such as *sad*, *mad*, and *frustrated*. By bringing puppets into the daily circle time, teachers can create a strong sense of community among children."[173]

So it's time to bring out the flannel puppets, the marionettes, and the sock puppets – as someone rightly said, "While the puppets sing and talk, our children listen."

Acknowledgements

It takes a village...

In so many ways, this book has been the work of many. I would like to thank the following people for being part of my village in helping me accomplish my dream.

My siblings, JP Rangaswami, Anant Rangaswami, Sreepriya Srinivasan, and my Amma, for always encouraging me, and for believing in me.

My sister, and literary agent, Jayapriya Vasudevan, thank you for everything. This book has happened because of you.

Somesh, for your support.

The Srinivasan Family at GEAR- thank you, Srini, Savi, Sunny, Madhu and Savera. Thank you for your friendship and love.

Deepa Joshi and Amitabh Sarwate, for pushing me to reach for the stars.

The Kirtane-Vanikar family, for your enthusiastic support!

Joma and Milind Uncle, for your unconditional love.

Ashwini and Vikram, for being there for me always!

Josie, my friend and supporter, who has encouraged me to keep writing.

Todd Hioki, my partner in crime in South Africa. Thank you for helping me see children through different lenses.

Phyllis and Derrick De Motta, for helping me believe that everything is possible!

Frona and Ted Kahn, for always being my champions!

Shelley, my dear, wise friend, for being my agony aunt!

My friends at TCS, especially Don Packham- for the endless cups of coffee, and for keeping me grounded.

My family at Pacific Oaks College and Children School who helped me become "the little engine that could!" Thanks, Pat Breen and Crystal Czubernat!

Holly Bruno, for showing me how to live life!

My dear editor, Ruchika, who has spent many sleepless nights trying to figure out what my words really meant. Thank you for helping me make this possible!

Ashwati, for making it presentable!

Ritesh, thank you for all the kerning and leading! Thank you for listening, and for all of the encouragement.

It takes a village.

Author Bio

Jayanti Tambe is the Executive Director of Early Learning at UCLA. She has also served as the Executive Director of Pacific Oaks Children's School. Prior to moving to Southern California, Jayanti served as the director of the Rainbow School and Pepper Tree School at Stanford University. She has taught courses on Child, Family, Community, Music & Movement, Supporting Dual Language Learners in a Multilingual Classroom, Health & Safety, Administration in Early Childhood Education, Business and Fiscal Management, and HR Administration in Educational Leadership, among others. Through her appointment by several national associations, institutes and universities, she has been widely accredited for her innovation in teaching practices

ENDNOTES

[1]Pica, R. (n.d.). Take it Outside! Retrieved from Early Childhood NEWS: http://www.earlychildhoodnews. com/earlychildhood/article_view.aspx?ArticleID=275

[2]Playing with... Loose Parts. (2011, Feb 14). Retrieved from Museum Notes: http://museumnotes.blogspot. in/2011/02/playing-with-loose-parts.html

[3]Jones, E. (2007). Teaching Adults, Revisited: Active Learning for Early Childhood Educators.

[4]Dalton, S. S., & Tharp, R. G. (2010). Standards for Pedagogy: Research, Theory and Practice. Retrieved from http://people.ucsc.edu/~gwells/Files/Courses_ Folder/documents/DaltonTharp.CREDE.pdf

[5]Bergland, C. (2013, Nov 15). Hand-Eye Coordination Improves Cognitive and Social Skills. Retrieved from Psychology Today: https://www.psychologytoday.com/ blog/the-athletes-way/201311/hand-eye-coordination-improves-cognitive-and-social-skills

[6]Joint Attention Without Gaze Following: Human Infants and Their Parents Coordinate Visual Attention to Objects Through Eye-Hand Coordination. (2013, Nov 13). Retrieved from PLOS ONE: www.plosone.org

[7]Bergland, C. (2013, Nov 15). Hand-Eye Coordination Improves Cognitive and Social Skills. Retrieved from

Psychology Today: https://www.psychologytoday.com/
blog/the-athletes-way/201311/hand-eye-coordination-
improves-cognitive-and-social-skills

[8]Huffman, J., & Fortenberry, C. (2011, Sept). Helping
Preschoolers Prepare for Writing: Developing Fine
Motor Skills. Retrieved from MBAEA (Mississippi
Bend Area Education Agency): https://www.mbaea.org/
documents/resources/Young_Children__Sept_2011_
Fine_Moto_B4C268611CA36.pdf

[9]Fine Motor Development. (n.d.). Retrieved from School
Sparks: http://www.schoolsparks.com/early-childhood-
development/fine-motor

[10]Fine motor skills - Infancy, Toddlerhood, Preschool,
School age, Encouraging fine motor development.
(n.d.). Retrieved from Psychology : http://psychology.
jrank.org/pages/247/Fine-Motor-Skills.html

[11]Coffey, L. T. (2014, Aug 1). Baby boy doll with realistic-
looking penis shocks some parents. Retrieved from
Today Parents: http://www.today.com/parents/doll-
penis-shocks-some-parents-1D80005572

[12]Coffey, L. T. (2014, Aug 1). Baby boy doll with realistic-
looking penis shocks some parents. Retrieved from
Today Parents: http://www.today.com/parents/doll-
penis-shocks-some-parents-1D80005572

[13]Dutta, S. (2013, Apr 30). How to Talk to Children about
Rape. Retrieved from The Wall Street Journal India:
http://blogs.wsj.com/indiarealtime/2013/04/30/how-to-
talk-to-children-about-rape/

[14]Teach your child the Underwear Rule. (n.d.). Retrieved from Council of Europe: http://www.underwearrule.org/source/text_en.pdf

[15]Cherry, K. (2014, Dec 20). What is Attachment Theory? - The importance of Early Emotional Bonds. Retrieved from About: http://psychology.about.com/od/loveandattraction/a/attachment01.htm

[16]Dolls and Doll Play - A new look at a familiar prop. (2004). Retrieved from Texas Child Care: http://www.childcarequarterly.com/summer04_story1a.html

[17]Dolls and Doll Play - A new look at a familiar prop. (2004). Retrieved from Texas Child Care: http://www.childcarequarterly.com/summer04_story1a.html

[18]Dorothy, G., & Singer, J. L. (n.d.). Reflections on Pretend Play, Imagination and Child Development (An Interview). Retrieved from Journal of Play: http://www.journalofplay.org/sites/www.journalofplay.org/files/pdf-articles/6-1-interview-relections-on-pretend-play.pdf

[19]Dolls and Doll Play - A new look at a familiar prop. (2004). Retrieved from Texas Child Care: http://www.childcarequarterly.com/summer04_story1a.html

[20]Hammond, C. (2014, Nov 18). The 'pink vs blue' gender myth. Retrieved from BBC: http://www.bbc.com/future/story/20141117-the-pink-vs-blue-gender-myth

[21]Wolchover, N. (2012, Aug 12). Why is pink for girls and blue for boys? Retrieved from Livescience: http://www.livescience.com/22037-pink-girls-blue-boys.html

[22]Thukral, E. G. (2002). Children in Globalising India Challenging our Conscience. Retrieved from HAQ Centre for Child Rights: http://www.haqcrc.org/publications/children-globalising-india-challenging-our-conscience

[23]Aina, O. E., & Cameron, P. A. (2011). Why does Gender Matter? Counteracting Stereotypes with Young Children. Retrieved from Southern Early Childhood: http://southernearlychildhood.org/upload/pdf/Why_Does_Gender_Matter_Counteracting_Stereotypes_With_Young_Children_Olaiya_E_Aina_and_Petronella_A_Cameron.pdf

[24]About William's Doll. (n.d.). Retrieved from http://www.charlottezolotow.com/willilams_doll.htm

[25]Allard, L. T., & Hunter, A. (2010, Oct). Understanding Temperament in Infants and Toddlers. Retrieved from Centre on the Social and Emotional Foundations for Early Learnin: http://csefel.vanderbilt.edu/resources/wwb/wwb23.html

[26]Gaias, L. M., Gartstein, M. A., Fisher, P. A., & Putnam, S. P. (n.d.). Cross-cultural Temperamental Differences in Infants, Children, and Adults in the United States of America and Finland. Retrieved from NCBI (National Center for Biotechnology Information): http://www.ncbi.nlm.nih.gov/pmc/articles/PMC3310888/

[27]Gaias, L. M., Gartstein, M. A., Fisher, P. A., & Putnam, S. P. (n.d.). Cross-cultural Temperamental Differences in Infants, Children, and Adults in the United States of America and Finland. Retrieved from NCBI (National

Center for Biotechnology Information): http://www.ncbi.nlm.nih.gov/pmc/articles/PMC3310888/

[28]Allard, L. T., & Hunter, A. (2010, Oct). Understanding Temperament in Infants and Toddlers. Retrieved from Centre on the Social and Emotional Foundations for Early Learning: http://csefel.vanderbilt.edu/resources/wwb/wwb23.html

[29]Boudinot, D. (n.d.). Violence and Fear in Folktales. Retrieved from La Trobe University: http://www.lib.latrobe.edu.au/ojs/index.php/tlg/article/view/31/35

[30]Jones, E. (n.d.). Giving Ourselves Permission to Take Risks. Retrieved from Exchange: https://www.childcareexchange.com/catalog/product/giving-ourselves-permission-to-take-risks/5020646/

[31]Mesure, S. (2014, May 24). When we stop children taking risks, do we stunt their emotional growth? Retrieved from Independent: http://www.independent.co.uk/life-style/health-and-families/features/when-we-stop-children-taking-risks-do-we-stunt-their-emotional-growth-9422057.html

[32]Jones, E. (n.d.). Giving ourselves Permission to Take Risks. Retrieved from http://ececompsat.org/docs/hsn-takingrisks.pdf

[33]Friedrich Froebel. (n.d.). Retrieved from Friedrich Froebel: http://www.friedrichfroebel.com/

[34]Maria Montessori (1870 - 1953). (n.d.). Retrieved from Women's Intellectual Contributions to the Study of Mind and Society: http://faculty.webster.edu/woolflm/montessori.html

[35]Armstrong, T. (n.d.). Multiple Intelligences. Retrieved from American Institute for Learning and Human Development: http://www.institute4learning.com/multiple_intelligences.php

[36]Backer, B. (n.d.). Manipulatives: Tools for Active Learning. Retrieved from Early Childhood NEWS: http://www.earlychildhoodnews.com/earlychildhood/article_view.aspx?ArticleID=123

[37]Lies: Why children lie, and what to do. (n.d.). Retrieved from raisingchildren.net.au: http://raisingchildren.net.au/articles/lies.html

[38]Tip Sheet: Lying. (n.d.). Retrieved from The Bair Foundation: Child and Family Ministries: https://www.bair.org/Portals/0/Images/foster%20parent%20resources/TIP%20SHEET%20-%20Lying.pdf

[39]Child Planning: A Treatment Overview for Children with Lying Problems. (n.d.). Retrieved from TherapyTools.US: http://www.therapytools.us/course_article.php?course_id=170

[40]Lying. (n.d.). Retrieved from Center for Effective Parenting: http://www.parenting-ed.org/handouts/lying.pdf

[41]Kennedy-Moore Ph.D, E. (2013, Jan 31). Imaginary Friends: Are invisible friends a sign of social problems? Retrieved from Psychology Today: https://www.psychologytoday.com/blog/growing-friendships/201301/imaginary-friends

[42]Asher, D. (2001, May). Dealing with Stealing. Retrieved from Parents Magazine: http://www.parents.com/kids/development/social/stealing/

[43]Asher, D. (2001, May). Dealing with Stealing. Retrieved from Parents Magazine: http://www.parents.com/kids/development/social/stealing/

[44]Drexler Ph.D, P. (2013, Mar 20). Why Kids Lie. Retrieved from Psychology Today: https://www.psychologytoday.com/blog/our-gender-ourselves/201303/why-kids-lie

[45]Moyer, M. W. (2014, May 16). Children Lie. Retrieved from Slate: http://www.slate.com/articles/double_x/the_kids/2014/05/children_lie_parents_should_teach_them_not_to_but_also_know_that_lying_is.html

[46]Levin, D. E. (2009, Feb 20). Beyond Banning War and Superhero Play Meeting Young Children's Needs in Violent Times. Retrieved from Education.com: http://www.education.com/reference/article/banning-war-superhero-play-children/

[47]Carlson, F. (n.d.). Rough and Tumble Play 101. Retrieved from Exchange: http://www.ccie.com/library/5018870.pdf

[48]Casper, V., & Theilheimer, R. (2010). Early Childhood Education: Learning Together. McGraw-Hill.

[49]King, M., & Gartrell, D. (2003, Jul). Building an Encouraging Classroom with Boys in Mind. Retrieved from Ebsco Host Connection: http://connection.ebscohost.com/c/articles/19142154/building-encouraging-classroom-boys-mind

[50]Perry, D. F., Holland, C., Darling-Kuria, N., & Nadiv, S. (2011, Nov). Challenging Behavior and Expulsion from

Child Care: The Role of Mental Health Consultation. Retrieved from Zero to Three: http://main.zerotothree. org/site/DocServer/32-2_Perry.pdf

[51]Perry, D. F., Holland, C., Darling-Kuria, N., & Nadiv, S. (2011, Nov). Challenging Behavior and Expulsion from Child Care: The Role of Mental Health Consultation. Retrieved from Zero to Three: http://main.zerotothree. org/site/DocServer/32-2_Perry.pdf

[52]Fox, M., & Vivas, J. (1984). Wilfrid Gordon McDonald Partridge. Retrieved from Mem Fox: http://www. memfox.com/wilfrid-gordon-mcdonald-partridge.html

[53]Graham, P. J. (2013, Jan 17). How do Children Comprehend the Concept of Death? Retrieved from Psychology Today: https://www.psychologytoday. com/blog/hard-realities/201301/how-do-children-comprehend-the-concept-death

[54]How Children Understand Death. (n.d.). Retrieved from Scholastic: http://www.scholastic.com/browse/ article.jsp?id=3754881

[55]Salek, M. E., & Ginsburg, M. M. (2015, Nov 21). How Children Understand Death & what you should Say. Retrieved from healthychildren.org: https://www. healthychildren.org/English/healthy-living/emotional-wellness/Building-Resilience/Pages/How-Children-Understand-Death-What-You-Should-Say.aspx

[56]Bosak, S. V. (n.d.). Benefits of Intergenerational Connections. Retrieved from Legacy: http://www. tcpnow.com/guides/intergenbenefits.html

[57]Bosak, S. V. (n.d.). Benefits of Intergenerational Connections. Retrieved from Legacy: http://www.tcpnow.com/guides/intergenbenefits.html

[58]Medoff, L. (2009, Jun 29). Preschool Potty Mouths: What to do about Bad Words. Retrieved from education.com: http://www.education.com/magazine/article/preschoolers-bad-words/

[59]Reece, T. (n.d.). How to handle a potty mouth. Retrieved from Parents: http://www.parents.com/toddlers-preschoolers/discipline/improper-behavior/potty-mouth/#page=1

[60]Smidl, S. L. (2014, June). My Daddy Wears Plucky, Ducky Underwear. Retrieved from naeyc: https://www.naeyc.org/files/naeyc/images/voices/11_Smidl%20v9-1.pdf

[61]Potty Talk: How Parents Can Discourage the Behavior. (2015, Nov 21). Retrieved from Healthy Children: https://www.healthychildren.org/English/ages-stages/toddler/toilet-training/Pages/Potty-Talk.aspx

[62]Derman-Sparks, L., & Edwards, J. O. (2010). Anti-Bias Education for Young Children and Ourselves. Retrieved from naeyc: https://www.naeyc.org/store/files/store/TOC/254.pdf

[63]Derman-Sparks, L., & Edwards, J. O. (2010). Anti-Bias Education for Young Children and Ourselves. Retrieved from naeyc: https://www.naeyc.org/store/files/store/TOC/254.pdf

[64]Bernstein, L. (2002). Understanding "It's Mine". Retrieved from Parents: http://www.parents.com/

toddlers-preschoolers/development/social/learning-to-share/

[65]The meaning and importance of pro-social behavior. (2012, Feb 21). Retrieved from sesameworkshop: http://www.sesameworkshop.org/our-blog/2012/02/21/the-meaning-and-importance-of-pro-social-behavior/

[66]Hyson, M., & Taylor, J. L. (2011, Jul). Caring about Caring: What Adults can do to Promote Young Children's Prosocial Skills. Retrieved from naeyc: http://www.naeyc.org/files/yc/file/201107/CaringAboutCaring_Hyson_OnlineJuly2011.pdf

[67]Should little kids be forced to share in Preschool? (2013, Apr 17). Retrieved from abc NEWS: http://abcnews.go.com/blogs/lifestyle/2013/04/should-little-kids-be-forced-to-share-in-preschool

[68]Education and Schools. (n.d.). Retrieved from UNICEF: http://www.unicefusa.org/mission/protect/education

[69]Segal, M. (2010, Jan 1). Organizing, Editing and Inspiring. Retrieved from Community Playthings: http://www.communityplaythings.com/resources/articles/2010/organizing-editing-and-inspiring

[70]Wilson PhD., R. (n.d.). Promoting the Development of Scientific Thinking. Retrieved from EarlyChildhood News: http://www.earlychildhoodnews.com/earlychildhood/article_view.aspx?ArticleId=409

[71]Chapter 10: Play and the Learning Environment. (n.d.). Retrieved from SAGE: https://uk.sagepub.com/sites/default/files/upm-binaries/53567_ch_10.pdf

[72]Stimulation Crucial to Development. (n.d.). Retrieved from Kids Growth: http://www.kidsgrowth.com/resources/articledetail.cfm?id=259

[73]Elkind, D. (n.d.). The Wisdom of Play/ How children learn to make sense of the world. Retrieved from Community Playthings: http://elf2.library.ca.gov/pdf/WisdomOfPlay.pdf

[74]Miles Ed.D, S. (n.d.). Exploration and Discovery !Creating an Enthusiastic, Exciting Classroom. Retrieved from Earlychildhood NEWS: http://www.earlychildhoodnews.com/earlychildhood/article_view.aspx?ArticleID=150

[75]Lindeman, K. W., & Anderson, E. M. (2015, Mar). Using Blocks to Develop 21st Century Skills. Retrieved from naeyc: http://www.naeyc.org/yc/files/yc/file/201503/YC0315_Blocks_Develop_21st_Century_Skills_Lindeman.pdf

[76]Sarama, J., & Clements, D. H. (2009). Building Blocks and Cognitive Building Blocks. Retrieved from Michigan Mathematics and Science Center Networks: http://mathscience.foxbrightcms.com/downloads/math__curriculum_support/building_blocks_and_cognitive_building_blocks_20111101_101612_1.pdf

[77]Sarama, J., & Clements, D. H. (2009). Building Blocks and Cognitive Building Blocks. Retrieved from Michigan Mathematics and Science Center Networks: http://mathscience.foxbrightcms.com/downloads/math__curriculum_support/building_blocks_and_cognitive_building_blocks_20111101_101612_1.pdf

[78]Anderson, C. (2010, Mar). Blocks: A Versatile Learning Tool for Yesterday, Today and Tomorrow. Retrieved from naeyc: http://www.naeyc.org/files/yc/file/201003/HeritageWeb0310.pdf

[79]MacDonald, S. (n.d.). Assessing Justin's Block Play. Retrieved from Earlychildhood NEWS: http://www.earlychildhoodnews.com/earlychildhood/article_view.aspx?ArticleID=136

[80]Jones, E. (n.d.). The Emergence of Emergent Curriculum. Retrieved from naeyc: https://www.naeyc.org/yc/files/yc/file/201203/Heritage_v67n2_0312.pdf

[81]Guha, S. (2007, Jul 26). Mathematics through Play. Retrieved from education.com: http://www.education.com/reference/article/Ref_Mathematics_Through/

[82]Seitz, H. J. (n.d.). The Plan: Building on Children's Interests. Retrieved from UNM Center for Development and Disability: http://www.cdd.unm.edu/ecln/PSN/common/pdfs/The%20Plan%20and%20Young%20Children%20March%202006.pdf

[83]Sprung, B. (1996, Jul). Physics is fun, Physics is important, and Physics belongs in the Early Childhood Curriculum. Retrieved from Southern Utah University: http://www.li.suu.edu/library/circulation/Gubler/flhd3900bbPhysicsIsFunPhysicsIsImportantFall08.pdf

[84]Kohn, A. (2001, Sept). Five Reasons to Stop Saying "Good Job!". Retrieved from Alfie Kohn: http://www.alfiekohn.org/parenting/gj.htm

[85]Bailer, K. (2003). Developmental Stages of Scribbling. Retrieved from Early Years: http://www.

earlyyears.org.au/__data/assets/pdf_file/0010/159724/
Developmental_stages_of_early_drawing.pdf

[86]Bongiorno, L. (n.d.). How Process Art Experiences
Support Preschoolers. Retrieved from naeyc: http://
www.naeyc.org/tyc/article/process-art-experiences

[87]Be Reggio Inspired: Learning Experiences. (2013, Mar
20). Retrieved from Let the Children Play: http://www.
letthechildrenplay.net/2013/03/be-reggio-inspired-
learning-experiences.html

[88]Duckworth, E. (2006). The Having of Wonderful
Ideas: And Other Essays on Teaching and Learning, 3rd
Edition. Teachers College Press.

[89]Encourage Learning. (n.d.). Retrieved from Smithsonian
Education: http://www.smithsonianeducation.org/
families/time_together/encourage_learning.html

[90]Nobleza, M. (2013, Sept 26). A Creativity-focused
Agenda for Early Childhood Education Policymaking.
Retrieved from The Huffington Post: http://www.
huffingtonpost.com/michael-nobleza/a-creativity-
focused-agenda_b_3992121.html

[91](n.d.). Retrieved from The Media League: http://www.
themedialeague.com/media/2776

[92]Edwards, M. (2011, Apr 11). Help your child develop
the "Crossing the Midline" skill. Retrieved from
North Shore Pediatric Therapy: http://nspt4kids.com/
parenting/help-your-child-develop-the-crossing-the-
midline-skill/

[93]Education and Schools. (n.d.). Retrieved from UNICEF: http://www.unicefusa.org/mission/protect/education

[94]Klein, L. G., & Knitzer, J. (2007, Jan). Promoting Effective Learning: What every Policymaker and Educator should know. Retrieved from National Center for Children in Poverty: http://www.nccp.org/publications/pub_695.html

[95]Cherry, K. (2015, Apr 6). Cognitive Development in Early Childhood. Retrieved from About: http://psychology.about.com/od/developmentalpsychology/ss/early-childhood-development_3.htm

[96]P.Heath. (2014, Apr 23). Insights from Piaget. Retrieved from education.com: http://www.education.com/reference/article/insights-piaget/

[97]Ages and Stages: Helping Children Develop Logic and Reasoning Skills. (n.d.). Retrieved from Scholastic: http://www.scholastic.com/teachers/article/ages-stages-helping-children-develop-logic-reasoning-skills

[98]Exploring Inquiry Learning in Early Childhood Education. (2011). Retrieved from Curriculum Research and Development Group/ University of Hawaii at Manoa: http://manoa.hawaii.edu/crdg/year-in-review/year-in-review-2011/exploring-inquiry-learning-in-early-childhood-education/

[99]Worth, K. (2010). Science in Early Childhood Classrooms: Content and Process. Retrieved from ECRP: http://ecrp.illinois.edu/beyond/seed/worth.html

[100]Bennett, H. (2006, Oct 3). Mirror Magic. Retrieved from Today's Parent: http://www.todaysparent.com/baby/baby-development/mirror-magic/

[101]Creating Early Learning Environments/ Info Practice Booklet. (2009, May). Retrieved from Saskatchewan Ministry of Education: http://www.education.gov.sk.ca/Default.aspx?DN=4de38060-953f-4922-9b9b-1d3bec94400d

[102]Boyle, R. (2012, Oct 1). We are all born scientists, study finds. Retrieved from Popular Science: http://www.popsci.com/science/article/2012-10/all-kids-are-junior-scientists

[103]Teaching your child to Identify and Express Emotions. (n.d.). Retrieved from CSEFEL: Vanderbilt University: http://csefel.vanderbilt.edu/familytools/teaching_emotions.pdf

[104]Teaching your child to Identify and Express Emotions. (n.d.). Retrieved from CSEFEL: Vanderbilt University: http://csefel.vanderbilt.edu/familytools/teaching_emotions.pdf

[105]Dissanayake, E. (1992). The Core of Art: Making Special. Retrieved from http://jcacs.journals.yorku.ca/index.php/jcacs/article/viewFile/16856/15662

[106]Wells, A. (n.d.). The Reggio Emilia Approach: A Social Constructivist Pedagogy of Inclusion. Retrieved from University of Manitoba: https://umanitoba.ca/faculties/education/media/Wells-09.pdf

[107]Danko-McGhee, K., & Shaffer, S. (n.d.). Looking at Art with Toddlers. Retrieved from Smithsonian: http://

www.si.edu/content/seec/docs/article-artwithtoddlers.pdf

[108]Kaufman Ph.D, S. B. (2012, Mar 6). The need for Pretend Play in Child Development. Retrieved from Psychology Today: http://www.psychologytoday.com/blog/beautiful-minds/201203/the-need-pretend-play-in-child-development

[109]The Importance of Play. (2010, Oct). Retrieved from Saskatchewan Rivers Public School Division: http://www.srsd119.ca/departments/teacherinformation/ILD/Kindergarten/importance_play.pdf

[110]Jean, P., & Barbel, I. (1969,2000). Psychology of a Child.

[111]The importance of Fantasy, Fairness, and Friendship in Children's Play. (n.d.). Retrieved from Journal of Play: http://www.journalofplay.org/sites/www.journalofplay.org/files/pdf-articles/2-2-interview-paley-fantasy-fairness-friendship.pdf

[112]The Importance of Pretend Play. (n.d.). Retrieved from Scholastic: http://www.scholastic.com/parents/resources/article/creativity-play/importance-pretend-play

[113]The importance of Fantasy, Fairness, and Friendship in Children's Play. (n.d.). Retrieved from Journal of Play: http://www.journalofplay.org/sites/www.journalofplay.org/files/pdf-articles/2-2-interview-paley-fantasy-fairness-friendship.pdf

[114]How To Handle Picky Eaters. (n.d.). Retrieved from Zero to Three: http://www.zerotothree.org/child-

development/health-nutrition/how-to-handle-picky-eaters.html

[115]Gadzikowski M.Ed, A. (n.d.). Story dictation: A Guide for Early Childhood Professionals. Retrieved from Chicago Metro AEYC: http://www.chicagometroaeyc.org/files/pdfs/STORYDICTATION.pdf

[116]Vygotsky. (n.d.). Retrieved from Child Studies: http://childstudies.livejournal.com/3759.html

[117]Vygotsky. (n.d.). Retrieved from Child Studies: http://childstudies.livejournal.com/3759.html

[118]Sternklar, D. (n.d.). Felt Stories in Storytime. Retrieved from UHLS: http://uhls.org/workshop_handouts/flannel_boards_presentation.pdf

[119]Enhancing Children's Language Development in Preschool Classrooms. (n.d.). Retrieved from Arizona State University: http://www.asu.edu/clas/icrp/research/Publication/Publication%20PDF%202.pdf

[120]Wang, S. S. (2009, Dec 22). The Power of Magical Thinking. Retrieved from The Wall Street Journal: http://online.wsj.com/news/articles/SB10001424052748703344704574610002061841322

[121]Popova, M. (n.d.). The Magic of Metaphor: What Children's minds Reveal about the Evolution of the Imagination. Retrieved from Brain Pickings: https://www.brainpickings.org/2013/08/19/james-geary-i-is-an-other-children-metaphor/

[122]Beneke, S. J., Ostrosky, M. M., & Katz, L. G. (2008, May). Calendar Time for Young Children: Good

intentions gone Awry. Retrieved from naeyc: https://www.naeyc.org/files/tyc/file/CalendarTime.pdf

[123]PRESS RELEASE: Heavily Decorated Classrooms Disrupt attention and learning in young children, according to new Carnegie Mellon Research. (2014, May 27). Retrieved from Carnegie Mellon University: http://www.cmu.edu/news/stories/archives/2014/may/may27_decoratedclassrooms.html

[124]Millar, E. (2013, May 9). How do Finnish Kids Excel without rote learning and standardized testing? Retrieved from The Globe and Mail: http://www.theglobeandmail.com/report-on-business/economy/canada-competes/how-do-finnish-kids-excel-without-rote-learning-and-standardized-testing/article11810188/

[125]Oxenbury, H., & Rosen, M. (1997). We're Going on a Bear Hunt. Oct: Margaret K McElderry Books. Retrieved from Amazon: http://www.amazon.com/Were-Going-Classic-Board-Books/dp/0689815816

[126]Aina, O. E., & Cameron, P. A. (2011). Why does Gender Matter? Counteracting Stereotypes with Young Children. Retrieved from Southern Early Childhood: http://southernearlychildhood.org/upload/pdf/Why_Does_Gender_Matter_Counteracting_Stereotypes_With_Young_Children_Olaiya_E_Aina_and_Petronella_A_Cameron.pdf

[127]Aina, O. E., & Cameron, P. A. (2011). Why does Gender Matter? Counteracting Stereotypes with Young Children. Retrieved from Southern Early Childhood: http://southernearlychildhood.org/upload/pdf/Why_Does_Gender_Matter_Counteracting_Stereotypes_

With_Young_Children_Olaiya_E_Aina_and_
Petronella_A_Cameron.pdf

[128]Dewar, G. (2009-2012). The Science of Toy Preferences in Children. Retrieved from Parenting Science: http://www.parentingscience.com/girl-toys-and-parenting.html#sthash.IeRrjyDF.dpuf

[129]Dorrell, A. (n.d.). Toys that Teach: Making age-appropriate choices. Retrieved from Earlychildhood NEWS: http://www.earlychildhoodnews.com/earlychildhood/article_view.aspx?ArticleID=678

[130]Liu, J. H. (2011, Jan 31). The 5 best toys of all time. Retrieved from Wired: http://archive.wired.com/geekdad/2011/01/the-5-best-toys-of-all-time/all/

[131]Encounters. (2010/11). Retrieved from Reggio Emilia: http://www.reggioemilia.org.nz/pdf/Encounters%20summer%202010_11.pdf

[132]Schirrmacher, R. (n.d.). Clay. Retrieved from Chicago Children's Museum: https://www.chicagochildrensmuseum.org/WorkingwithClay.pdf

[133]Schirrmacher, R. (n.d.). Clay. Retrieved from Chicago Children's Museum: https://www.chicagochildrensmuseum.org/WorkingwithClay.pdf
[134]Swartz, M. I. (2005, Mar). Playdough: What's Standard? Retrieved from naeyc: http://www.naeyc.org/files/tyc/file/TYC_V3N3_Swartz.pdf

[135]Zachry, A. (2012). Teaching Preschoolers to use Scissors. Retrieved from Parents: http://www.parents.com/toddlers-preschoolers/development/physical/teaching-preschoolers-to-use-scissors/

[136]Murphy, B. L., & Moon, R. (n.d.). Babies and their senses. Retrieved from Zero to Three: http://www.zerotothree.org/child-development/temperament-behavior/babies-and-their-senses.html

[137]Hughes, P. (n.d.). Benefits of Messy Play. Retrieved from More4Kids: http://baby.more4kids.info/2008/03/benefits-of-messy-play/

[138]Gopnik, A. (2010, Jul). How Babies Think. Retrieved from Alison Gopnik: http://www.alisongopnik.com/papers_alison/sciam-gopnik.pdf

[139]Klein, R. (2015, 3 29). Finland's Schools are Overhauling The way they do Things. Here's How. Retrieved from The Huffington Post: http://www.huffingtonpost.com/2015/03/28/finland-education-overhaul_n_6958786.html

[140]Jackson-Hayes, L. (n.d.). We don't need more STEM majors. We need more STEM majors with liberal arts training. Retrieved from The Washington Post: https://www.washingtonpost.com/posteverything/wp/2015/02/18/we-dont-need-more-stem-majors-we-need-more-stem-majors-with-liberal-arts-training/

[141]Murphy, B. L., & Moon, R. (n.d.). Babies and their senses. Retrieved from Zero to Three: http://www.zerotothree.org/child-development/temperament-behavior/babies-and-their-senses.html

[142]Wilkin, L. (2010, Jan). Use open-ended questions to improve kid's language skills. Retrieved from Columbus Parent: http://www.columbusparent.com/content/stories/2010/01/03/open-ended-questions-to-improve-language-skills.html

[143]Wilkin, L. (2010, Jan). Use open-ended questions to improve kid's language skills. Retrieved from Columbus Parent: http://www.columbusparent.com/content/stories/2010/01/03/open-ended-questions-to-improve-language-skills.html

[144]Hutchinson, M. (2015, Aug 15). Scaffolding Self-Regulated Learning in Young Children: Lessons from Tools of the Mind. Retrieved from Tools of the Mind: http://www.toolsofthemind.org/philosophy/scaffolding/

[145]Kochhar-Bryant. (2010). What does it mean to educate the whole child? Retrieved from SAGE: http://www.sagepub.com/sites/default/files/upm-binaries/34869_Kochhar_Bryant__Effective_Collaboration_for_Educating_the_Whole_Child_Ch1.pdf

[146]Developmentally Appropriate Practice (DAP). (n.d.). Retrieved from naeyc: http://www.naeyc.org/DAP

[147]Multiple Intelligences. (n.d.). Retrieved from American Institute for Learning and Human Development: http://www.institute4learning.com/multiple_intelligences.php

[148]Jennes, G. (1984, Apr 23). Don't Rush Your Child, Warns Psychologist David Elkind, or They (and You) Will Pay the Price. Retrieved from People: http://www.people.com/people/archive/article/0,,20087655,00.html

[149]Curwood, J. S. (n.d.). What happened to kindergarten? Retrieved from Scholastic: http://www.scholastic.com/teachers/article/what-happened-kindergarten

[150]Yenigun, S. (2014, Aug 6). Play doesn't end with childhood: Why adults need recess too.

Retrieved from nprED: http://www.npr.org/blogs/ed/2014/08/06/336360521/play-doesnt-end-with-childhood-why-adults-need-recess-too

[151]Zeng-tian, Z., & Yu-le, J. (2004). Some thoughts on Emergent Curriculum. Retrieved from http://www.edpsycinteractive.org/CGIE/yule.pdf

[152]Gross, C. M. (2012). Science Concepts young children learn through Water Play. Retrieved from Southern Early Childhood: http://www.southernearlychildhood.org/upload/pdf/Science_Concepts_Young_Children_Learn_Through_Water_Play_Carol_M_Gross.pdf

[153]Zeng-tian, Z., & Yu-le, J. (2004). Some thoughts on Emergent Curriculum. Retrieved from http://www.edpsycinteractive.org/CGIE/yule.pdf

[154]Education Theory: Constructivism and Social Constructivism. (n.d.). Retrieved from UCD: http://www.ucdoer.ie/index.php/Education_Theory/Constructivism_and_Social_Constructivism

[155]Education Theory: Constructivism and Social Constructivism. (n.d.). Retrieved from UCD: http://www.ucdoer.ie/index.php/Education_Theory/Constructivism_and_Social_Constructivism

[156]Stanchfield, J. (2007). What is Experiential Education. Retrieved from Experiential Tools: http://www.experientialtools.com/about/experiential-education/

[157]Chickering, A., & Ehrmann, S. C. (1996). Implementing the Seven Principles: Technology as Lever,. AAHE Bulletin, October, pp. 3-6.

[158]Theories: Theories of Learning. (n.d.). Retrieved from the spot... A Child's Museum: http://www.thespotmuseum.org/theories

[159]The irresistible classroom. (2014). Retrieved from Community Playthings: http://www.communityplaythings.co.uk/learning-library/training-resources/the-irresistible-classroom

[160]Scotty, J. (n.d.). About Maria Montessori. Retrieved from Children's Cornerstone: http://www.childrenscornerstone.com/about-maria-montessori/

[161]Puntambekar, S. (2009, Dec 23). Scaffolding. Retrieved from education.com: http://www.education.com/reference/article/scaffolding/

[162]Interest Learning Centers in Playschool. (n.d.). Retrieved from Preschool Plan It: http://www.preschool-plan-it.com/interest-learning-centers.html

[163]Rights for Every Child. (n.d.). Retrieved from UNICEF: http://www.unicef.org/rightsite/files/rightsforeverychild.pdf

[164]School Readiness. (n.d.). Retrieved from naeyc: https://www.naeyc.org/files/naeyc/file/policy/state/PSready98.pdf

[165]Rice, M. M. (2014, Feb 18). What is the teacher's role in supporting play in early childhood classrooms. Retrieved from VCU: http://www.ttacnews.vcu.edu/2014/02/what-is-the-teachers-role-in-supporting-play-in-early-childhood-classrooms/

[166]Be Reggio Inspired: Learning Experiences. (2013, Mar 20). Retrieved from Let the Children Play: http://www.letthechildrenplay.net/2013/03/be-reggio-inspired-learning-experiences.html

[167]Ohara, Y. (2013, Oct 11). Early childcare and education in India. Retrieved from Child Research Net: http://www.childresearch.net/projects/ecec/2013_13.html

[168]Bomengen, D. M. (2010, Sept 23). What is the "Whole Language" Approach to Teaching Reading? Retrieved from Reading Horizons: http://www.readinghorizons.com/blog/post/2010/09/23/what-is-the-whole-languagee-approach-to-teaching-reading.aspx

[169]Isbell, R. T. (Mar, 2002). Telling and retelling stories: Learning Language and Literacy. Retrieved from naeyc: http://www.naeyc.org/yc/files/yc/file/200203/Isbell_article_March_2002.pdf

[170]Glazer, S., & Burke, E. (1994). An integrated approach to early literacy.

[171]Paley, V. G. (1990). The boy who would be a Helicopter. Harvard University Press.

[172]Lao, J. (2015). Infant Language Development. Retrieved from Parenting Literacy: http://parentingliteracy.com/parenting-a-z/45-mental-development/97-infant-language-development

[173]Luckenbill, J. (n.d.). Circle Time Puppets: Teaching Social Skills. Retrieved from naeyc: http://www.naeyc.org/files/tyc/file/V4N4/Circle_time_puppets_teaching_social_skills.pdf